Feelgood

Feelgood

Alistair Beaton

Methuen Drama

Published by Methuen 2001

1 3 5 7 9 10 8 6 4 2

First published in 2001 by
Methuen Publishing Limited,
215 Vauxhall Bridge Road, London SW1V 1EJ

Methuen Publishing Limited Reg. No. 3543167

A CIP catalogue record for this book is available from the British Library

ISBN 0 413 77144 X

Typeset by SX Composing DTP, Rayleigh, Essex
Printed and bound in Great Britain by
Cox & Wyman Ltd, Reading, Berkshire

Feelgood premiered at the Hampstead Theatre, London, on 31 January 2001. The cast was as follows:

Eddie	Henry Goodman
Liz	Sian Thomas
Paul	Jeremy Swift
Asha	Amita Dhiri
George	Nigel Planer
Simon	Pearce Quigley
DL	Nigel Cooke

Directed by Max Stafford-Clark
Designed by Julian McGowan
Lighting by Johanna Town
Sound by Simon Baker

Characters

Eddie
Liz
Paul
Asha
George
Simon
DL

Setting

Act One
A suite in a grand hotel.

Act Two
Scene One: A room in a grand hotel.
Scene Two: A suite in a grand hotel (as Act One).
Scene Three: A party conference.

Act One

A large suite in the grand hotel of a British seaside town. The decor is dominated by gilt and chintz. Upstage centre long curtains frame the tall glass doors giving on to a balcony. Upstage right is the door giving on to the hotel corridor. Downstage right is a door through to the Prime Minister's rooms. Upstage left is the door to the en-suite bathroom.

There is a sense of stylish modern technology overrunning the fake Louis XV opulence of the suite: a couple of cables snake across the room, there is a television monitor on a steel and glass trolley, so the screen can be turned upstage when we don't need to see it. There are a couple of modern desks with typists' chairs, obviously imported specially into the suite. On one of the desks is an open laptop, on the floor beside it, a fax machine. On a small stand to one side is a printer. On the bigger desk there are a couple of coloured iMacs and two or three phones, at least one of them cordless. Nearby is a stylish hi-fi-CD player. There is a halogen lamp in burnished steel acting as a reading lamp for a Le Corbusier leather-and-steel recliner, both these items in stark contrast to the hotel decor. On a table with a cloth on it are vacuum flasks of tea and coffee, and silvery trays of sandwiches covered in clingfilm.

Music ('Feelgood' by James Brown).

*Lights snap up. Or curtain rises. We discover **Paul** sitting at the open laptop on the modern desk, and **Eddie**, who is some distance away from him, sprawled on the recliner, apparently relaxed but somehow always coiled and ready to pounce. It is a mid-afternoon. The music cuts out suddenly, maybe with a reverb.*

Paul (*reading from the laptop screen*) 'There will be other challenges facing us in the twenty-first century. But I can tell you now: the greatest challenge of all will be the challenge of change. And to those who –'

Eddie Ch. Ch.

Paul Sorry?

Eddie Ch. Ch.

Paul   Ch. Ch?

Eddie   Ch. Ch. Challenge of change. Don't like it.

Paul   It's alliteration.

Eddie   Yeah, bad alliteration. Challenge of change. Awful. It'll make him sound like he needs dentures.

Paul   Challenge of the new?

Eddie   Better.

Paul   But the greatest challenge of them all will be the challenge of the new. You're right. (*Types in the alteration.*) And to those who stand in the way of – the new – for whatever reason – I tell you this one, simple, undeniable truth: There is no going back.

Eddie   Nice.

Paul   Not too much like, you know, 'The lady's not for turning'?

Eddie   No harm in that.

Paul   Fine. Okay, now we go global, right? (*Back into text.*) But in the modern world, the challenge of ch – (*Correcting himself and typing it in.*) the challenge of the new is not something that can be faced by one nation on its own. Because a global economy brings with it global responsibilities.

Eddie   Yes. Good.

Paul   Let me tell you something. There are now six billion human beings on the planet. Today, 230,000 people will be born. Every day, the human race growing by the equivalent of the city of Sunderland. Every month –

Eddie   Sunderland.

Paul   Yes.

Eddie   Does it have to be Sunderland?

Paul   We've got two marginals in Sunderland.

Eddie   Oh . . . All right, then. Sunderland.

Paul   Every day, the human race growing by the equivalent of the city of Sunder –

Eddie (*impatient*)   Yes, yes.

Paul   Every month a London.

Eddie   That's good.

Paul   Every year another Germany.

Eddie   Yes. Good. Scary.

Paul (*reads*)   And shall I tell you how many of those children will grow up in the developing world?

Eddie   Forget children, here's better: newborn.

Paul   Newborn . . . Yes, it's more . . . um . . .

Eddie *and* **Paul**   Biblical.

Paul   Right. How many of those (*types in the correction*) . . . newborn will grow up in – (*stops, looks at* **Eddie**) No.

Eddie   No.

Paul   Newborns don't . . . grow up, somehow, do they?

Eddie   They don't. Stet children.

Paul (*types change*)   Stet children. How many of those . . . children will grow up in the developing world, where millions go hungry? Ninety-seven per cent.

Eddie *pours himself a glass of water and takes a tablet from a little foil pack in his pocket.*

Eddie   Needs more impact. Let me hear it again.

Paul   And shall I tell you how many of those children will grow up in the developing world, where millions go hungry?

Eddie   Long pause.

Paul (*types*)   Long . . . pause . . . Where millions go hungry . . . Ninety-seven per cent. And we cannot avoid the question: how are they to be fed?

Eddie *swallows the tablet, drinks the water, runs his hand through his hair. Silence.* **Paul** *looks over at him, uncertain of his reaction.*

Paul   Yeah?

Eddie   It's all a bit . . . you know . . .

Paul   A bit what?

Eddie   Well, there's not a lot of sunny uplands in there, is there?

Paul   Oh, I think he'll score highly on this. It's about being honest with the British people, making it clear that big global problems don't have easy answers, you know, treating them like adults.

Eddie (*sceptical*)   Ye-es . . . (*Ponders for a moment.*) Let's come back to this bit, eh?

In the distance, the faint sound of police sirens.

Paul   Sure. Okay. So we come out of the international stuff, whatever . . . and then . . . we lighten up with some spontaneous. It goes like this: First he pauses, looks round the hall, takes in the conference delegates, shakes his head, and grins.

Eddie   Sounds like last year's spontaneous. Which was embarrassing.

Paul   Yeah, well, he's not as good at spontaneous as he thinks he is.

Eddie (*testy*)   He's fine at spontaneous, Paul. The text wasn't right.

Paul   Sure. Whatever. So he smiles, and he says: You know, sometimes it feels like being Prime Minister is a job that's different from any other job. And in a way it is. Well, for a start, there aren't many other jobs where every week you get to meet three or four presidents, a couple of kings and queens, and a few hundred MPs. Except maybe if you're Charlotte Church.

Eddie (*stares hard at him for a moment*)   Did *you* write that?

Paul   Yeah.

Eddie   Go on.

Paul (*pauses, looks up at* **Eddie**)   It's a joke.

Eddie   Oh, good.

Paul   It's perfect, Eddie. It reminds people that he's a big player on the world stage, right? But at the same time it's self-deprecating, you know, just an ordinary guy doing an important job.

Eddie   I see. Is it funny?

Paul   Yeah. Definitely. It'll slay them.

Eddie's *attention is taken by the sirens, which are now louder. He wanders to the tall window, cranes to see something further up the street.*

Paul   Anyhow, there's a laugh, maybe some applause, I don't know, and DL goes very quiet and personal and . . . Are you listening?

Eddie (*still looking out*)   Yes.

Paul   And he says: But you know, it *is* different from any other job. Because it carries more responsibility than any other job. And sometimes it can be tough. Sometimes it means you don't have as much family time as you'd like, and you worry about the kids, and you worry about the mortgage, and you worry about –

Eddie (*turning back towards the room*)   Worry about the mortgage?! Give me a break! He doesn't have to worry about the mortgage!

Paul   Yes, well, *we* know that, but –

Eddie Everyone knows that! The whole population of the entire fucking universe knows that! Jesus! Have you been getting enough sleep?

Paul No. Sleep's not part of the job description, is it?

Eddie I thought maybe you'd been sitting up late writing your diary.

Paul I don't keep a diary.

Eddie Funny. I'd heard you did.

Paul The future. Worried about the future.

Eddie Better. Better than mortgage anyhow.

Paul And sometimes it means you don't have as much family time as you'd like, and you worry about the kids, and you worry about the future and you worry about the Deputy Prime Minister.

Eddie That's not bad. That might get a laugh.

Paul Do you think maybe it's a bit unfair?

Eddie (*grins*) Yes.

Paul Great. Okay . . . So then DL pulls the mood right back to earnest, right? And he says: But seriously, it's a privilege to be Prime Minister of this great nation. A nation of extraordinary talents. A nation of –

Asha *sweeps in from the corridor, mobile glued to her ear, papers and notes efficiently arranged under her arm. She crosses between the two men, bringing their conversation to a halt. As she speaks on her mobile she sticks a Post-it note on* **Paul**'s *desk.*

Asha (*on mobile*) Candyfloss?! Look, no way am I letting the Prime Minister walk down the pier eating candyfloss on camera, all right?

Paul A nation of entrepreneurs.

Asha (*on mobile*) Well, how about fish and chips? . . . Good. So he buys some fish and chips . . .

Paul   A nation of young people.

Asha (*on mobile*)   Make sure he's got some money on him, right? . . .

Paul   A nation of –

Asha (*on mobile*)   No, no plates, paper.

Paul   A nation of –

Asha   And he should ask for lots of salt and vinegar.

Eddie (*protesting the interruption*)   Asha . . . we're trying to –

Paul   A nation of –

Asha   That'll work great. Thanks. (*Switches off mobile.*)

Paul   Strong individuals.

Asha   God, the grief you go through to set up a halfway decent photo-opp.

Eddie   Oh that was a halfway decent photo-opp, was it?

Asha   For the last forty-five minutes, you two've been getting all your calls diverted to the Conference Centre. Now why's that necessary? Because it's frankly very irritating.

Eddie   Is it?

Paul   We're working on the Leader's speech, Asha.

Asha   Oh I get it. Everything else stops then, does it?

Eddie   Everything except you. Have you come across the concept of do not disturb?

Asha   It's hard for boys, isn't it? Not being able to keep more than one ball in the air at a time. Paul, I've been trying to page you for the last twenty minutes.

Paul (*looks down at his belt*)   Oh. Yeah. I switched off my bleeper.

Asha   You don't switch off your bleeper. Ever. All right?

Paul (*cowed*)   Okay okay. (*Mutters.*) Sorry. (*Leans down, fumbles with the pager on his belt.*)

Eddie (*half-aloud, as he walks back to his seat*)   Prime Minister walks down pier eating fish and chips. Fantastic. Hold the front page.

Asha (*to* **Paul**)   Okay . . . DL wants a new section inserted. On greenhouse gases. Something upbeat.

Paul   I see.

Asha   He feels there's too much doom and gloom around the issue. He wants to emphasise the upside.

Paul   Yes. Global warming. How it can be fun. That sort of thing.

Asha   You know what he means. Responsible economic growth. Respect for the environment doesn't mean cracking down on the two-car family. He wants to be proactive. He wants to come out fighting.

Eddie   What's brought this on?

Asha   The environment debate, Eddie. There's already been two speakers against the motion.

Eddie   Christ! How's that been allowed to happen? We agreed all contributions from the floor would be vetted by the Resource Centre.

Asha   They *were* vetted by the Resource Centre. But some delegates are going out there, throwing away the speech we cleared, and saying something completely different.

Eddie   Jesus, Asha, I lock myself away for a few hours to work with Paul on the big speech – or try to – and everything starts falling apart! It's a disaster. What's the point of setting up a resource centre to help delegates with their speeches if they can go out there afterwards and say what the hell they like?! (*Grabs jacket and moves towards door.*) I'd better get over there.

Asha   No. DL wants you working on the speech.

Eddie   Did he say that?

Asha   Yes.

Eddie   You sure?

Asha   Yes.

Eddie   Maybe I'll ask him myself.

Asha   I wouldn't. He's still spitting nails about the lunch-time bulletins. More footage of the demos outside than the speeches inside . . . Not what you'd call a PR triumph, is it?

Eddie   It was a slow morning. Fucking Euro. It's not exactly the Viagra of politics, is it? You try bringing the press to orgasm with a two-hour debate on convergence criteria.

Asha   Somebody should have realised that. Somebody should have known we wouldn't stand a chance against footage of People's Global Action or the League of Anarchists or whatever they're called.

Paul   Carnival against Capitalism, actually.

Asha   Anyway, they're extremely well organised, if you hadn't noticed.

Eddie   And pretty good at photo-opps.

Eddie *goes over to the monitor.*

Paul   Yeah, when I passed this morning, they had giant businessmen on stilts extruding plastic turds on to the heads of people dressed as third-world peasants. Quite imaginative, really. And I hear there's a breakaway gay group been attacking policemen, using pump action waterguns filled with pink dye.

Asha   Oh, do you like that?

Paul   Yes, I do quite.

Asha   I'll buy you a cowboy outfit for Christmas.

Paul   Thank you. That would be lovely.

Asha   Another point. DL wants his speech to have more laughs than last year. And bigger laughs. He wants you to liaise with some hot young gag writer.

Paul (*immediately apprehensive*)   Who?

Asha (*checks her notes*)   He's called . . . Simon Shadwick.

Paul   Simon Shadwick. What's he written?

Asha   Apparently he's a top TV comedy writer.

Paul   What's he written?

Asha (*checks notes again*)   It's very big at the moment . . . It's called . . . *Nobody's Perfect.*

Paul   *Nobody's Perfect?* Oh fucking hell. Have you seen it?

Asha   No, but it's a huge hit. DL's kids watch it.

Paul   Asha. Listen to me. *Nobody's Perfect* is a sitcom so toe-curlingly dire that when it comes on, cats have been known to hide behind the sofa. Drafting suicide notes.

Asha   Eight million viewers don't hide behind the sofa.

Paul   I'm sorry. I'm with the cats.

Asha   We checked him out. He's okay politically.

Paul   Oh, that's all right, then. Doesn't matter if his jokes are crap.

Asha   Well, Simon Shadwick it is, sorry. He's already on his way.

Paul   Oh God help us.

Asha   And DL wants you to draft up a passage on the yob culture.

Paul   Well what a fresh idea.

Asha Bit of iron fist, bit of velvet glove. Tough love. Hard choices. No rights without responsibilities. You know the line. He's jotted down a few thoughts of his own.

Paul Oh no.

*She drops a sheet of yellow lined paper on to **Paul**'s desk. He glances wearily at it. She gives a typed white sheet to **Eddie**.*

Asha Revised schedule for DL.

Eddie This is for me? Oh, thank you.

Asha (*checking her notes*) Now, tomorrow's real people. How many are they?

Eddie You mean ordinary people?

Asha (*shrugs*) Real, ordinary . . . How many?

Paul *goes back to working on the speech.*

Eddie Seven. I've given them twenty seconds each and told them not to stray from the text.

Asha Which is . . . ?

Eddie Basically, how each of them's seen one real measurable improvement in their life since we came to power . . .

Asha That's good.

Eddie Yes, I know.

Asha And at the end?

Eddie DL's to jump up from his seat and shake hands with them as they leave the platform. It shouldn't look too planned.

Asha And who are they? You know, what are they?

Eddie One nurse, one junior doctor, one millionaire, one head teacher, one graphic designer, one granny who's beaten loneliness and one bloke in a wheelchair. Four male, three female.

Asha   The millionaire, is he –?

Eddie   Yes. Self-made. Music business.

Asha   Good. Ethnic origin?

Eddie   Asian.

Asha   Brill. And the others?

Eddie   Um, one other Asian, one African-Caribbean, and four white.

Asha   The bloke in the wheelchair, is he –?

Eddie   No, he can shake hands, I checked that.

Asha *has been ticking off the items on her clipboard as they speak.* **Eddie** *idly picks up the schedule given to him by* **Asha***, glances over it.*

Asha   Okay. Next . . . (*refers to notes*) I want to check whether the timing for –

Eddie   I don't think everything I arrange needs 'checking', do you, Asha?

Asha   DL asked me to.

Eddie   DL asked you to check on the arrangements I have made?

Asha   Effectively, yes.

Eddie   Effectively, as in didn't ask you at all?

Asha   He trusts me, Eddie.

Eddie   He trusts you with his diary.

Asha   He trusts me with everything.

Eddie   I can't think why he'd want to do that, can you?

Asha   It's nothing to do with me being a woman, all right?

Eddie   Did I say that? Did I?

Asha   You don't need to. You're pathetic. (*Taking in* **Paul**.) You're all pathetic.

Paul   That's us. We're guys. We're pathetic. We're here. Get used to it. Hey.

Asha   Anyhow, Eddie, last year I dealt with all this conference stuff. Suddenly it's part of your brief. I thought you were press secretary? Or have I missed something here?

Eddie   I thought I was press secretary too. Which is why it's really very silly to have given you responsibility for photo-opps at Conference.

Asha   That was so you'd have more time to focus on the speech.

Eddie   I can do both. It works better when I do both.

Asha   There's something very wrong with you. I hear you followed a cleaner round the conference platform last night pointing out the bits she missed. And then sent her boss a memo.

Eddie   If I don't follow through on detail, people fuck up. That fish-and-chip walkabout really sucks.

Asha   If you don't like it, talk to DL.

Eddie   I might do that.

Asha (*looks at clipboard*)   Now, end of the day tomorrow. There'll be a helicopter waiting to take him to London, but DL wants – (*Her pager bleeps. She takes it from her belt, looks at it.*) Oh. He needs me over at the Centre.

Eddie   Oh dear. Then you'd better go, hadn't you?

Asha   Paul, page me when you've got a draft of the new stuff. (*To* **Eddie**.) Oh, that cleaner you complained about. She got fired. (*Leaves.*)

Eddie *turns back to* **Paul**, *who is looking over at him.*

Eddie   What are you staring at? People fuck up, they lose their jobs, that's just how it is.

Paul   Did I say anything?

Eddie   I can see you thinking it.

Paul   Amazing.

Eddie   I'd like that information to stay in this room.

Paul   You think Asha won't leak it?

Eddie *crosses to one of the monitors.*

Eddie   I know she won't. You'd be the only suspect. Let's get back to your text. I really want to make sure we don't repeat last year's mistakes.

Paul   My text? Last year there was hardly anything left of my text, after you and George had messed around with it.

Eddie   And DL. If I remember right, DL messed around with it a great deal.

Paul   That's different. He's Prime Minister. You don't expect him to be able to write a speech.

Eddie *switches on monitor and we see and hear (or possibly only hear) a snatch of a junior minister.*

Junior Minister (*on monitor*)   Not everything can be left to big business. We can do our own bit every day in small ways. Getting that loft insulation put in . . .

Eddie   Thank God for junior ministers.

Junior Minister (*on monitor*)   Walking to the shops occasionally instead of taking the car. Recycling those glass bottles. It's all a question of personal responsib –

Eddie *switches it off.*

Eddie   He'll go far.

Paul (*stares at the yellow handwritten sheet given him by* **Asha**, *reads:*)   Strong civic society . . . young offenders . . . curfews.

Oh God, it's depressing, isn't it? Why don't we just bring in King Herod as a curfew czar? He'd soon sort out them unruly little tots, wouldn't he?

A mobile phone rings. It plays the hook from 'All You Need is Love'. **Paul** *walks over to get the phone out of his jacket pocket.*

Eddie   We're not taking calls.

Paul   Yes, I know . . . (*Looks at read-out.*) Sorry, I've got to take this one. (*Answers phone.*) Steve, hi.

Eddie   I think that includes personal calls.

Paul (*turning his back on* **Eddie**) I can't talk now . . . I'll call you tonight . . . I can't be sure when . . . Steve, listen, I said –

Paul *is cut off. He switches off phone, sits down at the laptop again.*

Paul   Okay let's . . . Jesus . . . how am I meant to redraft this speech every ten minutes? And make curfews sound like a new idea? And be incredibly chirpy and upbeat about greenhouse gases, and then . . . and then, have to work in gags written by Simon fucking Shadwick?

Eddie   When did you last have an evening off?

Paul   Dunno.

Eddie   Maybe you need some free time.

Paul   Free time? What's that?

Eddie *comes up and stands behind him, while studying the laptop screen. He puts his hands on* **Paul**'s *shoulders, starts massaging them gently.*

Eddie   You got some leave booked after Conference, haven't you?

Paul   Yes.

Eddie   So what's the problem? (*Leans forward, types with one hand.*) A nation of opportunity . . . instead of . . . a nation of enterprise . . . Like that? Go away some place. No phones. No pagers. Leave the mobile at home.

Paul   Got my daughter coming to stay. What's wrong with a nation of enterprise?

Eddie   Sounds like a CBI convention. Half-term?

Paul   No, her half-terms are always with her mum. I don't get a look-in on half-terms.

Eddie   Just take her out of school then. Opportunity is good, you can't beat opportunity. Gives DL a hard-on, that word. Take her to Italy. I can arrange a villa in San Gimignano. What about 'a culture of achievement, not a culture of failure'? (*Leans over, types it in.*)

Paul   There's a court order. I'm not allowed to take her out of the country without Teresa's permission.

Eddie   Which she of course will not give you.

Paul   Which she of course will not give me. And this time Teresa's really larding it – stopping off at Euro-Disney on the way home.

Eddie   They're in France?

Paul   Yes . . . I quite like 'culture of achievement'.

Eddie   Good.

Paul   And now Teresa's found God I'm scared she's going to brainwash the kid. Last time I saw her, she told me Jesus was angry with me for leaving Mummy.

Eddie   That Jesus can be such a bitch.

Paul   It's hard. You know what an ex can be like. (*Looks round at* **Eddie**.) God, yes, you definitely know what an ex can be like.

Eddie, *obviously displeased, steps back.* **Paul** *registers the upset.*

Paul   Sorry. Not my business. If it's any comfort, when I saw her, I thought she was looking awful.

Eddie   When was this?

Paul   When I saw her? Yesterday.

Eddie (*surprised*)   Yesterday? She's here? Covering Conference?

Paul   I assume. I thought you always combed through the lists of accredited journalists?

Eddie   Four hundred of them here this year, Paul. Even I have to delegate a bit. It's not her usual beat, is it?

Paul   What is her usual beat these days?

Eddie   Oh you know, human rights in Kosovo, kids starving in Scunthorpe, asylum seekers dying in Dover, basically all the fun stories.

Paul   I don't see her byline much any more.

Eddie   You wouldn't. Not unless you read *Red Rostrum*.

Paul   I can't say I often get round to reading *Red Rostrum*.

Eddie   That's all right, not many people do. Poor Liz. From national broadsheet to *Red Bollocks*, not a great career curve, is it? (*Brightly changing subject.*) Okay. Time to sexy up those bits on the economy. (*Grabs a pen and clipboard.*) Let's make two lists . . . (*Draws a line.*) . . . on the left, key concepts . . . and on the right . . . memorable phrases . . . You do the memorable phrases.

Paul   Meaning I'm not trusted with the key concepts?

Eddie   Okay, okay. You do the key concepts, I'll do the memorable phrases.

Paul   Fine . . . (*Thinks.*) I'm better at memorable phrases.

Eddie   Let's just do it, eh, Paul?

George *bursts in through the corridor door. His hair is mussed, his tie askew, and his grey suit has a large pink stain on it.*

George   Shit! Shit, shit, shit! What kind of bloody country do we live in?! Will you look at this! (*Indicates stain.*) Look at it! Have you any idea what this suit cost me?!

Eddie   What happened, George?

George   Pursued down the front by a posse of poofters firing pink water guns.

Paul (*trying hard not laugh*)   Oh dear.

George (*wiping at stain*)   It's like every malcontent on the planet's come here for a week by the seaside.

Paul   Carnival against Capitalism.

George   Oh is that what it is? Well, that'll explain why I saw two transvestites on stilts having sex with each other. Or whatever it is transvestites do together.

Paul   Well, if it's done on stilts, it's an achievement.

George   And I'm starving. Hardly had a thing since breakfast. The restaurants have all put up their shutters! Because of some bloody GM protestors. Have you noticed how pale and ugly they all are? Those people aren't against genetically modified food, they're just against food! And they've been here all fucking week! In considerable numbers! Clogging up half the town. Couldn't somebody insert the terminator gene into them or something?

*He goes over to a tray of coffee and sandwiches, grabs some food, crosses to **Paul**'s desk.*

So. How's the big speech shaping up?

Paul (*pointedly*)   Trying to work on it, George.

George *ambles about and sounds off – he is not drunk, but it's clear he's had a couple of drinks.*

George (*picks up a vacuum coffee jug*)   Ah, coffee. Good. On draft two hundred and twenty-nine yet? Ha! Last year we finished it, oh, when was it, five in the morning on the day of the speech?

Eddie *is leaning over* **Paul***'s shoulder, spooling up on the rest of the speech.*

Paul   Six thirty actually, George.

George   Yes, that was a tough one. (*Picks up a couple of sandwiches.*)

Paul   I think you went to bed around three.

Eddie *gestures for* **Paul** *to give up his seat.* **Paul** *does so.*

Eddie   Let me get at this.

Eddie *starts making deletions and amendments on the screen.*

George (*bites into sandwich*)   You know, there's a cruel irony about these sandwiches. Here we are, close to the throbbing heartbeat of power. Anything we want can be ours. Well, just about anything. Not unreasonably, the electorate probably picture us sipping a glass of pretty decent Puligny-Montrachet as we toy languidly with a plate of seared scallops. And what's the grim reality? For the last three days it's been nothing but ham sarnies and fizzy fucking water.

Paul   Is that what you had last night?

George *crosses to the steel-and-leather recliner, sits on it.*

George   Eh?

Paul   You know, is that what they got for their five hundred quid a plate? Ham sarnies and fizzy fucking water? As Minister for Cabinet Coordination you presumably felt it was your sacred duty to be there.

George   I'm not talking about the fund-raising dinner, Paul. Cheesed off because you weren't there?

Paul   No. I wouldn't want to be there, as a matter of fact.

Eddie (*without looking up from the laptop*)   Yes you would. I'd rather you didn't sit on my recliner, George.

Paul   He's got a thing about it.

Eddie   I've got a thing about it.

George (*not getting up*)   Some would describe it as decadent.
Importing your own recliner for the duration of Conference.

Eddie   Would they?

George   You must admit, it is taking things a bit far. I
mean, none of us likes this overblown chintz stuff (*indicates
the suite*) that passes for luxury in provincial hotels. But I'd
have hoped you'd be able to drag yourself away from
minimalism for a few days, Eddie, without going into a
coma. What does this sort of thing cost, by the way?

Eddie   Too much for it to have your fat arse on it,
George.

George   You're a very rude man.

Eddie (*fiercely*)   Just fucking well get off it!

George *jumps up, rattled.*

George   Why do you have to be such a pain, Eddie?
Can't you ease up a bit? If you had the occasional drink
you'd probably be a bit more of a fun person.

Paul   I wouldn't bet on it.

George   I need a Jimmy Riddle.

George *crosses to the bathroom door, goes in, closes the door. We
hear the door being locked.*

Eddie   When did you last hear that expression – a Jimmy
Riddle?

Paul   In an Ealing Comedy?

Eddie   Not that he's actually Jimmy Riddling in there.
Well, he might be Jimmy Riddling in there, but Jimmy
Riddling is not the primary purpose of his visit.

Paul   Cocaine?

Eddie   Oh no. If you offered George a mirror and a razor, he'd probably start shaving. No, no. Hip-flask filled with vodka.

Paul   I did wonder.

Eddie   He imagines vodka can't be detected on the breath. A common misapprehension. Right. Memorable phrases. How about: um . . . a high-skill, high-income economy . . . (*writes*) . . .

Paul   Get skilled, or . . . get something-or-othered.

Eddie   Yes, that's good. So my message to you is: Get skilled or get . . .

Paul   Screwed.

Eddie   No.

Paul   Stuffed.

Eddie   No.

Paul   Scared.

Eddie   No.

Paul   Scorched.

Eddie   No.

Paul   Scuppered.

Eddie   No. How about: left behind?

Paul   Get skilled or get left behind?

Eddie   Yes.

Paul   Oh boring! I like get skilled or get screwed.

Eddie   You can't have the Prime Minister standing up in front of Conference telling people to get screwed!

Paul   I don't know. Reflects what he really feels about them, doesn't it? What's more, it's bold, clear, demotic, populist, and engagingly laddish.

Eddie   Yobbish, more like. Hey, hold on. That's it. This is good. A phrase that links economic success with being tough on crime.

Paul   Yeah? Like what?

Eddie   Try this. Try this for size. Right. Ready? A job culture, not a yob culture.

Paul   A job culture, not a yob culture.

Eddie   A job culture, not a yob culture.

Paul   That's fucking brilliant. Yeah! Zizzzz! (*They do a Michelangelo finger-to-finger routine.*) That's great. Says so much, doesn't it?

Eddie   Yeah. It says: Get skilled or get screwed.

The bleeper on each person's belt goes off at the same moment. **Eddie** *and* **Paul** *simultaneously go through the same routine of taking it from their belt, looking at it.*

George (*off*)   Oh bloody hell!

The bathroom door flies open and **George** *rushes in, holding his bleeper, and stuffing a hip flask back into his pocket. He hurries to monitor, grabs the remote, points it at screen, stabs buttons.*

George   What channel's got the feed from the Conference floor?

Eddie (*taking the 'remote' away from him*)   That's a telephone, George.

Eddie *picks up real remote, points it, switches on monitor. The audience cannot see the screen of the monitor, but the sound can be clearly heard.* **Paul**, **Eddie** *and* **George** *stand upstage of the monitor, facing downstage as they watch the proceedings. The first sound we hear is of disorder: cheers, applause, catcalls, etc. Through it we hear the voice of an ordinary delegate making a speech.*

Voice of Delegate (*female*)   . . . the prospect of a planet laid waste by Frankenstein food. The prospect of biotech

companies enslaving the farmers of the third world, the
prospect of new genes being let loose in the environment.

George   There's no escape, is there?

Voice of Chair   Will you wind up your remarks, please,
delegate?

From the floor of the hall come roars of protest against the chair.

Various Delegates   No! No!
Give her more time!
Let her speak!
Give her a chance (*Etc.*)

George   Oh hell!

Voice of Delegate   Delegates! New genes means new
species, which will escape into the environment . . . with
effects on the human race that nobody –

Voice of Chair   Your time's up, delegate!

From the floor come even louder shouts.

Various Delegates   No! No! No!
No it isn't!
We want to hear her! (*Etc.*)

Eddie *looks around, grabs a set of headphones with an attached mike
in front.*

Eddie (*to* **Paul**)   Connect me. Fast.

Paul *punches a number into a device which is attached by a wire to*
Eddie'*s headphone and mike.*

George (*watching monitor*)   Good God!

Voice of Delegate   This debate has been rigged!
(*Applause.*) Ordinary delegates haven't been given the
opportunity to express their views.

There are roars of applause and support.

Various Delegates   Right!
Exactly!
Hear hear!
You tell 'em!
Let's have a proper debate! (*Etc.*)

George   Stupid girl.

Eddie   Hurry it up, Paul . . .

Paul   You're through.

Eddie (*into mike, softly but very intently and clearly*)   Lily. It's Eddie. If you can hear me, scratch your nose . . . right. (*Watching screen.*) No, don't do that . . . don't put your hand up to your earpiece . . . It's our little secret.

George *looks back and forward from screen to* **Eddie**, *trying to figure out what's going on.*

Eddie   Okay. First. Switch the cow's microphone off . . .

Voice of Delegate   What's happened to democratic debate in this party?

Various Delegates   Exactly!
Yeah! Control freaks! (*Etc.*)

Eddie   Switch it off!

Voice of Chair   I'm switching your microphone off, delegate . . .

From the floor of the hall we hear a mixture of applause and catcalls.

Various Delegates   No! No!
Boooo! Boooooooo!
It's a fix!

Voice of Chair   I'm switching your microphone off.

Eddie   Well, do it then!

Voice of Delegate   This is a travesty of democracy. This is a travesty of democ – ! (*Her voice abruptly disappears, maybe can be heard very faintly in the background.*)

Eddie   Good. Now go for reference back.

Voice of Chair   I'm . . . I'm . . . I'm going to ask the proposers of this motion to agree to reference back.

There are shouts of dissent.

Various Delegates   No! No!
Fix! Fix!
Don't agree!
No reference back! (*Etc.*)

Eddie   For further consideration . . .

Voice of Chair (*struggling over sounds of dissent*)   For further consideration.

Eddie   By the policy forum.

Voice of Chair   By the policy forum.

There is more shouting from the floor.

Various Delegates   No! No!
Boooooooo! (*Etc.*)

Eddie   Don't touch the earpiece! You want everyone to know? . . . You're all right . . . let the shouting die down a bit . . . Uh-oh.

Rebel Voice (*male, a bit off-mike*)   We don't want reference back, we want a vote on this motion! (*Sounds of support.*)

Various Delegates   Yes! Yeah!
Give us a vote! (*Etc.*)
Hear hear!

Voice of Chair   Leave the platform, delegate . . . I'm asking you to leave the platform.

George   He's got the chair's microphone. It's anarchy down there! God, it's like the days of fucking Militant!

Rebel Voice (*on mike*)   Delegates! Comrades!

Eddie   Lily . . . Lily!

George   Comrades! He said comrades!

Eddie   Lily, can you hear me! (*To* **Paul**) It's breaking up. She can't hear me!

Rebel Voice   Comrades . . . !

Various Delegates   Yeah!
Hooray! (*Etc.*)

George   Twice!

Eddie   Shut up, George! Lily, you're voting on reference back. Lily, don't let him keep the mike like that! Lily! Shit!

George   Will you look at that?! Where's security when you need them?

Rebel Voice   We have a right to a vote and we're going to have a vote!

Roars of applause and support.

Various Delegates   Yes! Hooray! (*Etc.*)

Eddie   Lily! Paul, I've lost the connection!

Paul   No, look, she's dropped the earpiece.

Eddie   Oh you stupid old bat. Shit! . . . (*Peers at screen.*) Well, hide it, for God's sake! . . . that's better.

Rebel Voice   All those in favour of the motion, please show! . . . (*Sounds of Lily in background trying to recapture the mike.*)

George, **Eddie** *and* **Paul** *go silent as they watch anxiously.*

Rebel Voice   Against? . . .

George (*mutters*)   Oh God . . .

Rebel Voice   The motion is defeated.

Sounds of uproar.

Various Delegates (*cheer*)   Yeahhhhhhhhh!

Voice of Chair   We're . . . we . . . I'm . . . Delegates . . .
Conference will be adjourned for ten minutes. Ten minutes.

Various Delegates   Well done!
We showed em. Yeah!!!!

Eddie *takes off mike and headphones, throws them on table.*
George *glumly switches off the monitor.*

Eddie   Open these phone lines.

Paul *punches some figures into the master phone.*

Eddie   Okay, Paul, get going on that GM section. I want
three versions to offer him. (*Counts on fingers.*) One robustly
proactive, GM is good, GM is the future. One that backs off
a bit: you know, we make our judgement in the national
interest when the facts are known – same bollocks as the
single currency, okay? And one that doesn't mention GM at
all.

Paul (*going to laptop*)   Right.

Eddie   Now. Let's close this down before it lifts off.

George   It's not going to look pretty on the Six o'Clock, is
it?

George *moves towards the door to corridor.*

Eddie   I think you'll find there will be very little of it on
the Six o'Clock, George.

George   You'll be lucky. By the way, when did you
organise that . . . that little trick . . . (*points to his own ear*) . . .
you know, direct line to chair of Conference?

Eddie   Can't think what you're referring to, George.

George   I see. Fine. Well, you can rely on me.

Eddie   I fucking hope I can, George.

George   Going to my room to change.

Eddie   Always prioritise.

George (*looks down at suit again. Wipes at it*)   Anarchist bastards. (*Leaves.*)

Eddie (*to* **Paul**)   Is Richard still around or has he gone back to London?

Paul   BBC Richard, *Daily Mail* Richard, *Guardian* Richard, Reuters Richard, or Branson?

Eddie   BBC.

One of the other phones rings. **Eddie** *waves at it, indicating* **Paul** *should answer it.* **Paul**, *irritated, crosses to the phone.*

Paul   Went back to London last night.

Eddie *punches in a number on a cordless phone.* **Eddie** *paces around as he speaks.*

Paul (*into phone on cord*)   Yeah?

Eddie (*into cordless*)   Hi, give me Richard, will you?

Paul (*into phone*)   What?

Eddie (*into cordless*)   It's Eddie . . .

Paul (*into phone*)   Oh no.

Eddie (*into cordless*)   You tell him it's Eddie, darling, and he'll come out of the meeting.

Paul (*into phone*)   Where? . . . Oh Christ. (*To* **Eddie**.) It's the Deputy PM. There's a problem.

Eddie   What is it this time?

Paul   His train's broken down.

Eddie   Aw no. Isn't he meant to be on the front for a photo-opp?

Paul   Yes. He's unveiling a new eco-friendly electric car at four.

Eddie   Where is he now?

Paul   Wilmere Station.

Eddie (*looks at watch*)   He might just make it. Tell him we'll send a car.

Paul (*into phone*)   Jim. We'll send a car . . . hmm . . . I see . . . yeah . . . Has anyone spotted you yet? . . . Right . . . (*To* **Eddie**.) There's about two hundred stranded passengers, no buses or anything. Jim's hiding behind a newspaper. If he's whisked away in a big car, it won't look good. He's worried the press'll get hold of it.

Eddie   I'll make sure they don't.

Paul (*into phone*)   Eddie'll make sure they don't . . .

Eddie (*into cordless*)   I'm holding for Richard.

Paul (*into phone*)   Yeah . . . all right . . . (*To* **Eddie**.) He says, can you make it a small car? Something that looks like a minicab . . . and maybe not too new . . .

Eddie   Tell him we'll send him the smallest, shabbiest, shittiest old car we can find.

Paul (*into phone*)   He says don't worry. Sure . . . Outside the station . . . discreetly . . . sure. (*Puts phone down. Picks it up again.*)

Eddie (*into cordless*)   Richard, how're you doing? Listen, you got a running order for the Six o'Clock yet? . . . Yeah, right, I'll hold.

Paul (*into phone*)   Get me transport, will you? (*To* **Eddie**.) Do we have any shabby old cars?

Eddie   Shouldn't think so.

Paul   Would it be better if he took a local minicab?

Eddie   No. Last time he did that the driver sold the story to the *Mirror*.

Paul   Oh yeah . . . (*recalls the headline*) . . . 'Bogeyman! Deputy PM Picks Nose at Eighty Miles an Hour!'

Eddie *gives him an impatient look.*

Paul   Sorry. Loved that headline.

George *re-enters from the corridor, having changed into a different suit.*

George   Can you believe it? A Filipino maid burst into my room while I was changing. Didn't even have enough English to say 'sorry'.

Eddie (*into cordless*)   Richard? Yeah? The environment debate? . . . No, not a vote. That wasn't a vote . . . There's no way you can say the leadership lost the vote when it obviously wasn't a valid vote, so I don't call that much of a story . . . You're not serious! – What, you're going to lead on it? . . . Responsible journalism?! . . . That's not what I'd call it, I'd call it anti-government bias . . . Listen, Richard, if the BBC thinks . . . yeah . . . yeah . . . I hear you . . .

Paul (*into phone*)   Who's that? Sarah, hi, you took your time, didn't you? Yeah, well, this is urgent. Look, I need someone to pick up the Deputy Prime Minister . . . he's at . . . no, his train's broken down . . . (*Sotto voce, under* **Eddie***'s next speech, which is delivered downstage of* **Paul***:*) Wilmere Station. W-I-L-M-E-R-E . . . that's right . . . Yes. Now, this needs to be discreet. Yes. There's a lot of pissed off passengers. So he wants it low-key . . . Yeah . . .

Eddie (*into cordless*)   Richard, of course I'm not interfering with editorial control . . . Listen, there were big announcements made here today, big new initiatives on health. You're not telling me that a few flat-earthers banging on about GM foods is a bigger story than two billion pounds more for the NHS, are you? . . . Hey, Richard, that's . . . well, no . . . I'm not, no, I'm just . . .

Paul (*into phone, irritated*)   Well, what's the smallest, oldest car you've got?

As well as talking on the phone, **Eddie** *is registering what* **Paul** *is saying.*

Eddie (*into cordless*)   Don't give me that, Richard, I'm not buying that . . . It's a clear case of BBC bias . . . Oh I think I can promise the Prime Minister will share my view . . . I suspect questions will be asked about your role, Richard, and at a very high level . . . You can interpret it any fucking way you like . . . (*Puts the cordless down.*) Asshole! (*Stares at* **Paul** *in silence for a moment.*)

Paul (*into phone*)   Is that the smallest you got? . . . Yeah, okay. Thanks, Sarah. (*Puts phone down.*)

George   How come we've got a Deputy Prime Minister who can't get anywhere on time?

Paul   Nobody can get anywhere on time any more, George. It's called an integrated transport policy.

Eddie   Paul, go over to the Centre, will you, and get me all you can on that idiot woman who wrecked the environment debate. You know, does she fuck dogs, has she had a sex-change op, has she ever been on holiday to Cuba, et cetera et cetera. I want the full dustbin on her. Enough to give the red-tops a hard-on. And I want the files on those two who spoke against the motion.

Paul   I can access membership files from here.

Eddie   Yes, but I want you to dig for dirt on the mad harpy. Ask around a bit.

Paul   I don't think that's my job. And anyhow, if you want me to write three drafts of the GM section for –

Eddie   Just do what I'm asking, there's a good lad.

George   It isn't really the best use of his talents, is it, Eddie?

Eddie   Stay out of this, George, please.

Paul   I'm fed up being used as an office boy!

Eddie   Think of it as multi-skilling.

Paul   And I don't like your way of dealing with dissent.

Eddie   Oh God, it's conscience time.

Paul   I'm hired as a speech writer, Eddie. I'm hired as a special adviser. I'm hired as a strategist. I'm not part of your thought police!

Eddie   Shall I tell you what you are, Paul? You're a smart kid with a good degree and a very high salary. A backroom boy with attitude. A wonk. You're an egghead with street cred. A damned good speechwriter. But just a little bit emotional. And that's the bit that mars your judgement. That's the bit you're going to have to watch. How's Steve, by the way?

Paul   Steve?

Eddie   Steve. He called you earlier, didn't he?

Paul   He's fine.

Eddie   Oh good. Nip round to the Boots stall while you're there and get me some vitamin C tablets, there's a good boy. Half-gram, chewable, orange flavour. Say they're for me and you'll get them for free.

Paul   Yeah. Okay. (*Leaves.*)

George   You ought not to alienate him at this stage, Eddie. We need him to finish writing tomorrow's big speech.

Eddie   He won't walk, don't worry. He's an ambitious little shit. Anyhow, I could make life too unpleasant for him.

George   Got something on him?

Eddie (*meaningfully*)   Got something on everyone, George.

George   Including me?

Eddie   Oh yes.

George (*laughs, suddenly stops*)   Such as?

Eddie   Now . . . We have a story to kill. Don't want the sad bastards from today's environment debate all over our

TV screens tonight, do we? (*Picks up a phone, punches in a number.*) Eddie here. Give me transport, and hurry up.

George   We'll . . . we'll just have to hope there's something big enough to push us out of the headlines. An earthquake somewhere. Or a plane crash, perhaps. Yes, a plane crash would get us off the hook.

Eddie   Great idea, George. I'll have two jumbos put on collision course right away. (*Into phone.*) Transport?

George *lumbers over to* **Paul***'s laptop, sits down, scrolls up on the draft speech.*

Eddie   . . . Is that Sarah? It's Eddie . . . that car for Jim, what model you sending? . . . Well, that's ridiculous . . . the man's Deputy Prime Minister for God's sake, I'm not having him being driven around in a Fiesta . . . I want something top of the range. (*With one phone in his hand, he starts on-hook dialling on another phone using the other hand.*) A Daimler? Perfect . . . Yeah, okay. Now hurry it up, will you? Thanks. (*He puts that phone down, as other one is answered.*) It's Eddie again. Put me through to Richard. This is urgent . . . Richard? Uh? . . . Well, I'm glad it's no longer the lead, but . . . second item? . . . Well, second item isn't much of an improvement, is it? . . . No . . . no . . . Just listen, Richard, will you? I've got something better for you . . . Yeah, it's exclusive . . . Only I'll expect the environment debate to fall right down your agenda . . . And anyhow, this is a lot sexier than the environment . . . Okay, here it is: get a film crew over to Wilmere train station. Now . . . Just do it . . . Trust me . . . Wilmere. Byeee. (*To* **George**.) That should make our Jim look pretty silly. Filmed sitting in the back of a fucking huge Daimler, as he zooms off to unveil an environmentally friendly car. In which we anyhow do not wish to invest public money.

George   I don't think you should say that.

Eddie   Say what, George?

George   This passage here, about transparency. (*Reads.*) 'And let me tell you this. Your government believes in transparency. In openness. Our commitment to the best of the new is based upon an open and honest assessment of the technology –'

Eddie   It's maybe a bit lumpy. Paul's still working on it.

George   No, no, that's not what I mean. Listen . . . (*Reads.*) 'an honest and open assessment of the technology. No secret experiments. No secret meetings with the biotech companies. No secret crop trials.' (*Looks up at* **Eddie**.) I don't think you should ask the Prime Minister to say that.

Eddie   No, that's okay. There's a public record of the fact that we've had meetings with the biotech companies, there's just no public record of what was said. So technically, it's completely correct to say there have been no secret meetings. Because although what was said in the meetings is secret, people do know that we have the meetings. Ergo, we've had no secret meetings. (*Into mobile.*) Gaynor, get back to me, will you? I think I'm about to have an interesting angle on the GM nutter who jumped the platform. I'll keep it just for you, if you're nice to me. (*Talks into mobile.*) Ring Caroline.

George   No, I mean, you shouldn't say 'No secret crop trials'.

Eddie   Why not? Hi, Caroline! Eddie here, it's not your voice-mail I need, sweetheart, it's you! What do you do at ITN all day, have lunch? Get back to me soon, I got something big just for you. (*Puts phone down. To* **George**.) Why not?

George   It's just . . . well, it seems like a hostage to fortune, that's all.

Eddie *punches a code into the master phone to divert all calls. There is a pause as* **Eddie**, *suddenly wary and alert, comes over and circles* **George** *menacingly.* **George** *tries to avoid his eye.*

Eddie   Why does it seem like a hostage to fortune, George?

George   Um . . . well . . .

There is silence for a moment. **George** *rubs at his brow nervously.*

Eddie   You're not suggesting there have been secret crop trials, are you, George?

George   No.

Eddie   I mean, as Minister for Joined-up Government, you wouldn't be party to some secret arrangement about crop trials, would you?

George   Absolutely not.

Eddie   So what's the problem with saying 'No secret crop trials'?

George   Just, you know, precautionary.

Eddie   You're not really cut out for political life, are you, George? That's the problem with the Prime Minister parachuting old friends into the Cabinet office. Politically, you're naive. You haven't been through the rough and tumble of getting elected. You don't see problems coming. You don't have . . . you don't have antennae. And of course you're a rotten liar.

George   I find this all very offensive, Eddie. If you're going to –

Eddie   George. I know about the secret crop trials.

George   Eh?

Eddie   On your land.

George   Oh.

Eddie   You really need to learn to lie better, George.

George   Maybe I should take lessons from you.

Eddie   It wouldn't be a bad idea. You think DL embarks on something like this without talking it over with me first?

George   Yes, I suspect it happens more often than you'd like to believe.

Eddie   Don't fuck with me, George. You may be the PM's pal from way back, but when it comes to hard politics, we all know whose judgement he trusts. I'm not in this as his friend, George, I'm in this because I'm good.

George   You've always been jealous of my closeness to him.

Eddie   Not jealous, George. Worried by it. You're his Achilles heel. You've got no political nous. You wouldn't spot a scandal if it came up and sat on your face.

George   You do have a disgusting turn of phrase sometimes, Eddie.

Eddie   I know why he went for it, of course. Nearly all the GM crop trials were being destroyed by saboteurs. He was getting desperate. So you volunteered your private estate.

George   Yes.

Eddie   Four hectares of genetically modified maize were then secretly planted on your land. Fair summary?

George   Well . . . essentially . . . yes.

Eddie   Right. So you, me and DL knew about it. Although you didn't know that I knew about it. Right?

George   Yes.

Eddie   And now, suddenly, it's become, in your words, a 'hostage to fortune' to say again in public what we've already said in public. I can only conclude, George, that you believe there's been a leak.

George   Not exactly a leak, Eddie. But there have been some developments that you don't know about.

Eddie   But now you're going to tell me.

George   Yes . . . First, well . . . it wasn't exactly maize that was planted.

Eddie   Maize, wheat, corn, who cares?

George   It was hops.

Eddie   Hops? What, the stuff you make beer with?

George   Yes.

Eddie   Why hops?

George   I thought it wouldn't be noticed so easily.

Eddie   Why's that?

George   On my estate, they've been growing hops for hundreds of years. It's a local tradition.

Eddie   God, George, you sound as if you're landed gentry. 'On my estate' . . . the power of a life peerage, eh? Go on.

George   Now, as you may or may not know, hops are vulnerable to an infection known as verticillium wilt.

Eddie   Verticillium wilt? Sounds a bit like –

George   Brewer's droop, yes, yes. Quite an old joke, that. It's an infection that's wiped out millions of hectares of hops in the past. There's nothing you can do to stop it. Unless, of course, you could develop a genetically modified form of hops . . . resistant to the verticillium wilt.

Eddie   This would be commercially valuable?

George   Very.

Eddie   Which is the real reason you wanted the hops.

George   I . . . thought there could conceivably be . . . future commercial spin-offs, yes.

Eddie   And that's why you didn't tell anyone.

George   I told DL, of course. He knows it's hops (*Thinks.*)
If it were to come out . . . do you think one could argue that
hops is a harvest, rather than a crop? So when we said 'No
secret crop trials' we weren't . . . really . . . misleading the
public?

Eddie   No.

George   No.

Eddie   Why? Is it going to come out, George?

George   Christ. I hope not.

Eddie   Meaning it might?

George   Well, I think there could be a journalist on to it.

Eddie   Who?

George   Don't know. But in my village . . .

Eddie   You own the village too, now, do you?

George   In the village, I gather someone's been hanging
around the Lamb and Flag, asking questions.

Eddie   What kind of questions?

George   I don't know.

Eddie   Well, for example, were they asking 'Do you have
Old Scraggles Winter Warmer on draught?' Or were they
asking 'Excuse me, what's the quickest way to the field with
the government's secret crop trials in it?'

George, *with shaking hand, rubs his eyes.* **Eddie** *watches him
with cold detachment, assessing his next move.*

Eddie   You're not telling me the whole story, are you,
George?

George   It's . . . Eddie. It's bad.

Eddie   How bad?

George   Very bad.

Asha *enters, rattled.*

Asha   I've been saying it for two years now. We need a full-time conference organiser. A high-flyer. Someone from industry. Fifty-two weeks a year. With their own team. Doing nothing else but preparing for Conference. It's turned into amateur night over there. (*To* **Eddie**.) I've spoken to DL – who's deeply pissed off, by the way – and he agrees that you've got too many responsibilities. So what I've suggested for next year's Conference is that you –

Eddie   Shut up. Shut up and sit down.

Asha, *taken by surprise, sits down on the edge of the recliner.*

Eddie   Not there!

She stands up again. **Eddie** *walks over to her.*

Now listen. I don't care about next year's conference. I don't care about what you have or haven't said about me to DL. I don't care about your squalid little power games.

Asha   I'm not playing power ga –

Eddie (*putting a finger on her lips*)   Shhhh! I will care about these things again about half an hour after Conference ends. I might even care about them a great deal. Right now, I only care about making sure the rest of Conference goes brilliantly. And is perceived to go brilliantly. To that end, you and I need to work together. Because we have the same aims. We believe in the same things. We're not doing this for us. We're doing it for DL. We're both very very good at our jobs, and that's why we're here. Now. Did he bawl you out?

Asha   Yes. He was unbelievably vile.

She starts to cry a little. **Eddie** *puts his arm around her.*

Eddie   We've all been through that at one time or another. It's just his way.

Asha   I know.

Eddie   But it's still a horrible experience.

Asha   Yes.

Eddie   And I know how it feels.

Asha   Yes . . . Thanks, Eddie.

Eddie   Your make-up . . . there. (*Points, almost touches.*) Needs fixing.

Asha   Oh. (*Wipes at her mascara.*) Have I made it worse?

Eddie (*smiles*)   Yes.

Asha   Be right back.

Eddie   Sure.

He watches smiling as she crosses to the bathroom, and enters. The moment the door closes behind her, the smile disappears and he picks up the phone.

(*Into phone.*) Page Asha, will you? DL wants her over at the Conference Centre right away. Thanks. (*Puts down phone, looks over towards bathroom door.*)

George   I can't believe how stupid I've been.

Eddie (*holding up hand*)   Shhh! I can. (*Keeps looking at bathroom door.*)

A few seconds pass.

Asha (*off*)   Shit!

A couple more seconds pass. The bathroom door flies open and **Asha** *rushes out, bleeper in hand.*

Asha   Sorry, Eddie. DL wants me over at the Conference Centre right away.

Eddie   Aw. There's no escape, is there?

Asha   Right. I'll get back here soon as I can.

Eddie   Whenever. Not a problem.

Asha *leaves.* **Eddie** *waits for a second to make sure she's gone. Then he advances on* **George**.

Eddie   Tell.

George *goes over to the coffee/drinks trolley, searches around while* **Eddie** *takes a pack of silver-foil tablets out of his pocket, pops out a couple, chews them.*

George   I need a drink.

Eddie   There's fruit juice, mineral water, tea or coffee.

George   Yes . . . (*Pours a fruit juice, tastes it, expresses his disgust.*) I couldn't order an Armagnac from room service, could I? Okay, never mind, forget it.

Eddie   George . . .

George   A cognac would do.

Eddie   It's the leader's speech tomorrow. If there's anything to be closed down, we're going to have to close it down fast. If a new speech needs writing from scratch, we're going to have to write it pretty damn quick.

George   Yes. Right. Okay. Sorry . . . Well . . . the hops were harvested . . . and then, and then they should have been destroyed. A few samples to go to the labs, but basically, they should have been destroyed.

Eddie   Should have been . . . ?

George   Well, to be honest, one field of hops looks very much like another.

Eddie   Oh Christ, you destroyed the wrong hops?

George   Not me, personally, you understand. But yes, there was a bit of a muddle, and the wrong field was destroyed.

Eddie   And the GM field, the one that wasn't destroyed?

George   It was harvested. Nobody noticed the mix-up at the time.

Eddie   And then?

George   It got . . . You know, sent to the local brewery.

Eddie   You mean, it was made into beer?

George   Hops is only one component in beer. What happens is, you boil up the –

Eddie   I don't need the recipe. Did it end up in the beer?

George   Yes. It's a little local brewery. Just a couple of dozen barrels.

Eddie   Go on.

George   And then, this beer . . . which everyone thought was normal beer . . . got served in my local . . . As . . . beer . . . does.

Eddie *pauses, considers.*

Eddie   So . . . the secret trials led to a number of people unwittingly consuming genetically modified beer . . .

George   Yes.

Eddie   And you didn't think any of this was worth telling me?

George   The point is, what do we do now, Eddie? I think we need a plan. In case it comes out.

Eddie *ponders for a moment, while* **George** *sweats.*

Eddie   Didn't you stand up in the Lords and tell the House there were no secret trials?

George (*quietly*)   Yes.

Eddie*'s pleasure in* **George***'s possible downfall shines through.*

Eddie   Oh well, then, that's it. Lying to Parliament. Always a hard one to massage away, George.

George   Yes.

Eddie   What was the name of the company involved in the trials on your land?

George   Progenitor.

Eddie   Progenitor. Do you have any shares in Progenitor?

George   I have a wide portfolio of investments, Eddie.

George *has taken out the little silver hip flask. He unscrews the top.*

Eddie   Do you have any shares in Progenitor?

George   They're in a blind trust.

Eddie   That's not going to help much, George. We all know about blind trusts. Any other connection with Progenitor?

George *swigs at the hip flask, chokes a little.*

Eddie   I'll take that as a yes, shall I?

Off, there is an explosion. Then another one, louder.

George   What was that?!

This time there are flashes of coloured lights vaguely visible through the balcony doors.

What's going on?

Eddie   I think you'll find it's fireworks.

George   What, at this time of day? . . . God almighty!

Eddie   Fireworks, George.

George   But what for?

George *heads for the balcony, pulls the curtains aside, just as the biggest bang of all is heard, and parabolas of coloured lights are glimpsed in the sky. He opens the balcony doors. The sound of the fireworks is louder. We hear crowd noises and some sirens.*

Eddie   Publicity stunt by the street people . . . George?

But **George** *makes to go on to the balcony.* **Eddie** *pursues him.*
George *goes out on the balcony.*

Eddie   You're not planning to jump, are you?

George (*from balcony*)   Would you care?

Eddie   Yes. I need more information from you.

Eddie *also goes out on to the balcony. There is another bang and
more lights. The doors are all but closed and the curtains fall back
behind them. The suite is left empty for maybe five to ten seconds. Then
there is a knocking on the door from the corridor. After a moment, the
door opens and* **Simon***, chewing gum, cautiously enters, looks around
nervously.*

Simon   Hello-o . . . ? Anybody home? . . . Hello-o? Oh.

*He realises there is nobody there. He closes the door behind him, comes
into the suite. He is wearing a leather jacket and carrying a briefcase.
He has a few newspapers under his arm.*

*He checks out the room, puts stuff down on recliner, puts jacket over
back of recliner. He wonders what to do with gum, finally decides to
stick it under recliner. He checks out desks, takes things and occupies
upstage desk. He clears a space, takes out a notebook and pen. He
reads. He smiles appreciatively. He reads more. He laughs his
distinctive braying laugh.*

Haaaaaaaaaaaa!

*He thinks hard. He gets up. He paces. He has an idea. His face lights
up, he snaps his fingers. He writes down a gag in his notebook. He
reads it.*

Final proof came through last week when it was revealed
that the leader of the opposition uses one. Haaaaaaaaaaaaa!

*Shaking his head with pleasure he repeats his tagline as he wanders
over to the recliner.*

The leader of the opposition uses one! Oh yes, Haa!

*He sits down on recliner. He wipes the tears of laughter from his eyes.
He sighs. He works on another gag, can't get it. He looks around, sees*

door. Still puzzling over gag, and with pad and pen in hand, he goes over to it, knocks, opens door, sees it's the bathroom.

Ah-ha!

He disappears into the bathroom, we hear the door lock behind him. The suite remains empty and silent for maybe ten seconds. A couple more bright bursts of fireworks can be faintly seen from the balcony doors, and the sound of firework explosions is heard again. Then silence again. Then from the bathroom we hear an identical burst of the same braying laugh.

(*Off*)   Haaaaaaaaaaaa!

*A moment later, a mobile phone (***Paul****'s) starts ringing – the refrain from the Beatles 'All You Need is Love'. After two or three seconds of this, the balcony doors open, and* **George** *re-enters from the balcony, followed by* **Eddie**.

Eddie   So it's not on your register of interests.

George   No. Anyhow, there isn't any money in it. They provide me with a flat in central London, and pick up the tab for the occasional foreign trip, that's all.

Eddie   Oh, that's all?

George   We don't all live like monks, Eddie.

Eddie (*irritated by the ringing*)   Why can't Paul take his mobile with him? . . . (*Passes the desk laid out by* **Simon**, *glances at it, frowns.*) Whose is all this stuff?

George (*not interested*)   No idea.

Eddie *sees* **Simon***'s things on the recliner, throws them on the floor. He goes to* **Paul***'s desk, picks up the mobile, looks for the off-switch, see the read-out of the number.*

Eddie   We expecting anything important from France?

George   Eh? Don't know.

Eddie *stares at the read-out, the phone still ringing.*

Eddie   It's not a Paris number . . . (*Presses the answer button. Into mobile, curtly.*) Paul's phone . . . He's not here at the moment . . . No, I can't . . . Because I don't have time to take personal messages . . . Ah . . . Right . . . Where are you? . . . Ah. How bad is it? . . . I see . . . (*Takes pen and pad.*) . . . What hospital? . . . Right . . . Got it . . . yes . . . sure . . . and the number? (*Writes.*) . . . Okay. I'm putting it on his desk now . . . By tonight? But . . . yes, there's a direct flight from London, I think, but . . . Yes. (*With concern.*) Of course . . . Teresa, I'm really, really sorry to hear this. Your little girl will be in our prayers tonight. Yes. Goodbye. (*Switches it off.*) Shit! (*Throws mobile viciously at sofa, paces about a bit.*) Paul's kid's in hospital. Just outside Lyons. Car accident. Leg broken in three places. Needs metal pins inserted. Being operated on tonight. Fuck! . . . Brilliant timing, eh?

Eddie *ponders a moment more, then takes the note he's written, tears it into little pieces, and throws it in the bin.*

George   You can't do that!

Eddie   He can get over there soon as Conference is finished. It's not as if it's life-threatening, is it?

George   Seems a bit brutal.

Eddie   George. We're going to need Paul. Thanks to you. So don't come at me with the moral outrage stuff because it doesn't suit you. (*Picks up mobile, looks at it.*) Oh Christ, last-caller display. (*Hits the mobile against the heel of his shoe.*) Shit. Still there. (*Puts it on floor, stomps on it, walks away to continue conversation with* **George**, *but after two paces it starts playing a wonky version of its ringing tone: stuck on the last five notes – 'Love is All You Need'.*) Would you believe it?!

Eddie *goes back to mobile, jumps up and down on it until it's smashed.* **George** *looks on in silent apprehension.* **Eddie** *sweeps up the broken pieces, puts them into a folder, takes the folder up to balcony. On his way upstage, there is a final dying beep from the mobile. He throws the remains of the phone from the balcony.*

Eddie (*shouts down*)   Sorry!

He comes back downstage to **George**, *sits near him.*

Okay. Let's talk strategy.

George   Strategy? Eddie, you haven't heard the full story.

Eddie   There's more?

George   It gets worse.

Eddie   I find that hard to imagine, George.

George   Well, it . . . Right. The thing is . . . the hops . . . well, I mean, drinking the beer appears to have . . . some . . . side effects.

Eddie   The people who drank the beer got ill!

George   Not ill exactly . . .

Eddie   They're dead?

George   No, no . . . not dead. The women were fine, it didn't seem to affect any women. Though of course they don't drink as much beer, so –

Eddie   And the men?

George   This strain of hops, it's created – I mean I don't really understand the technology of this, Eddie, but . . . you know how some GM plants have a genetically altered antibiotic attached, which acts as a sort of marker . . . ?

Eddie   Go on . . .

Simon (*off, not so loud or long as last time*)   Haaaaaa!

Eddie *and* **George** *half-register the sound, dismiss it.*

George   In much the same way, apparently, this new strain of hops uses a genetically altered hormone. Which . . . it rather appears . . . has an . . . well, it has an unfortunate effect on the male body.

Eddie   How unfortunate?

George   Well, it does rather look as if . . . as if . . . as if most of the men . . . some of the men who drank this beer went on to . . .

Eddie   Went on to what, George?

George   I find this very hard to say.

Eddie   Just say it.

George   They grew breasts.

Eddie   They grew breasts?

George   Yes.

Eddie   The men?

George (*exploding*)   Well, of course, the men, Eddie! The women have already fucking well got breasts, in case you hadn't noticed!

Upstage of them, the bathroom door opens and **Simon** *enters, looking down at his notebook and shaking his head in silent admiration of his completed gag. They don't notice his presence. He suddenly clocks the other two men, freezes. Then he decides to go over and greet them.*

Eddie (*ignoring the insults, keeps trying to grasp the facts*)   The men who drank the GM beer developed breasts?

Simon *flinches as he hears this, drops his plan to greet them.*

George   Well . . . not all of them.

Eddie   Only some of them.

George   Yes.

Eddie   How many?!

George (*misunderstanding, he gestures to his chest*)   Well, two, of course.

Eddie   How many men!

Simon, *anxious, is about to say something, changes his mind, retreats a little, isn't sure what to do.*

George Nobody knows exactly. I gather several have been to their doctor. Some of them were a bit upset.

Eddie No, really?! Got depressed, did they? Suffering from PMT perhaps? Shit. Okay. Let's stay calm, let's stay focused. Let's think this through. It's not as if we have to withdraw something from the market, we're talking one-off here. So . . .

George Ah.

Eddie You did say just a little local brewery? A few dozen barrels?

George Absolutely. Right. Just a few dozen barrels. Initially.

Eddie There's no danger of this being licensed, is there?

George It's been licensed.

Eddie It's been licensed?

George Yes.

Eddie For commercial use?

George Yes.

Simon *begins to tiptoe back towards the bathroom.*

Eddie But I thought –

George We fast-tracked it. Washington was on the phone twice a day. The biotech companies were getting twitchy about the European market . . .

Eddie Are you saying . . . that this beer is on general sale . . . ?

George Was. I managed to get it withdrawn. Had to call in a few favours, I can tell you, Eddie. But it was on sale at . . . well, at quite a lot of pubs.

Eddie For how long.

George Um . . . just over three months.

Eddie   In how many pubs?

George   Quite a few, I'm afraid.

Eddie   How many?

George   About fourteen thousand.

Eddie   Oh good God.

Eddie *gets up, paces.* **Simon** *ducks down behind the monitor, aware that this is something he ought not to be hearing. The audience should still be able to see his face.*

George   There isn't a minibar in here, is there?

Eddie   How many people know?

George   About the hops?

Eddie   About the breasts. If a story comes out that's just about secret crop trials on your land, it's only you that's fucked. If it's about men growing tits, I think the entire government's fucked, don't you?

George   I don't think anyone's put two and two together. The local GP's a pal of mine. Had supper with him. That's when he told me about the cases.

Eddie   How many's he seen?

George   He's seen seven. Another GP in the next village has seen two. Two patients, that is. Not two . . . (*Indicates breasts.*) And presumably there are others who're . . . well, you know, it's quite embarrassing, I imagine. They wouldn't all proudly rush to their doctors to flaunt their . . . mammaries, would they?

Eddie *leans on the monitor.* **Simon** *gulps with fear.*

Eddie   Your GP friend. What's he put it down to?

George   He's not sure. Something in the water. Oestrogen from the pill. Or maybe too many fried chicken takeaways . . . It's been happening in other countries, you know. Apparently in some lakes in North America the male fishes are all turning a bit girlie, and I don't think anyone's going to start thinking the fish've been at the beer, are they? No, in this case, I really don't see how anyone's likely to make the connection. Even the brewery doesn't know they used the wrong hops.

Eddie   That's something, I suppose.

Eddie *moves way from the monitor.* **Simon** *can breathe again. There is a moment of silence.*

George   Apparently there's also some shrinkage of the genitalia.

Simon *and* **Eddie** *both wince.*

George   General feminisation.

Eddie   The party that turns men into women. Not a great election platform, is it?

Simon *(gets up)*   Are you sure you people need a comedy writer?

Eddie *stares at* **Simon**.

Eddie   Who the fuck are you?

Simon *stands up, tries to regain some sort of dignity.*

Simon   Hi. Simon Shadwick. *(Offers a handshake, which is ignored.)*

Eddie   What?

Simon   Simon Shadwick. Writer of *Nobody's Perfect?*

Eddie *stares blankly.*

Simon   You booked me.

Eddie   How long have you been around?

Simon   Oh, I've been writing professionally for quite a few years –

Eddie   Not around like . . . around. Here.

Simon   Um . . . well . . . I came in, then, um . . . then I went to the bathroom and then I . . . look, I promise I won't tell anyone.

Eddie   Oh Christ. (*To* **George**.) He's heard everything.

Simon   Not everything. But I got the gist. (*Indicates breasts*.)

Eddie   Okay, Samuel, you –

Simon   Simon.

Eddie   You sit down, Simon (*Pointing at recliner*.) Not there!

Simon   Please. Don't worry. You can trust me. I'm actually a member of the party.

Eddie   That's all I needed.

Simon   I'd like to do whatever's best for the party.

Eddie (*dismissively*)   Yes, yes.

Simon   If you'd prefer me just to disappear, I'll –

Eddie (*quickly*)   No! You're not going anywhere! . . . Just . . . relax . . . and um . . . you won't be making any phone calls, will you, Sam – Simon?

Simon   No, I don't think so . . .

Eddie   Have you got a mobile?

Simon   No. There's some evidence that they cause brain damage.

Eddie   Really? (*To* **George**.) The journalist. If it was a journalist. We've got to –

Simon   Yes. Final proof came through last week when it was revealed that the leader of the opposition uses one.

Simon *looks around, expecting appreciation for his 'joke'.*

Eddie (*blankly*)   Yes . . . I imagine he does . . . (*To* **George**.) The journo who was asking questions at your local pub. We've got to establish whether –

Simon   Sorry. That was inappropriate. I mean, I know you people have got, like, big deal problems on your hands.

Eddie   Right. (*To* **George**.) First. Do we know for sure it was a journo?

George   Well, apparently she showed someone a press pass, so presumably . . .

Eddie   It's a woman?

George   Yes.

Simon   Of course, some say there is no deadlier weapon than laughter.

Eddie *turns to give* **Simon** *a look of withering contempt.*

Simon   Sorry. I'll just take a back seat and work on a few ideas. (*In Mae West impersonation.*) Put me on the back burner, boys, I'll be hot when you're good and ready. Or should I say, I'll be good and ready when you're hot?

Eddie   Just shut up, okay?!

Simon (*with hurt dignity*)   Okay. Fine. Understood.

Simon *retreats, sits down on a chair.*

Eddie (*to* **George**)   Anyone remember what she looked like?

George   Who?

Eddie (*impatiently*)   This female journalist!

George   Haven't really pursued that. Didn't want to seem too interested.

Eddie   Got a number for the pub?

George   Yes, here somewhere . . . (*Rummages in jacket pockets.*) Or is it still in my other suit? Hang on . . .

George *hauls out diaries and notes and bits and pieces from his inside pockets, which irritates* **Eddie**. **Asha** *enters.*

Asha   Somebody's pissing me about. DL hadn't paged me at all. It's not my idea of a joke.

Eddie   Mine neither. Got that number yet, George?

George (*looking in notebook*)   I think I jotted it down in here . . . no, no, I tell a lie.

Asha   You checked out the latest focus group returns? Not good. They see him as someone who's failed to deliver. 'All mouth and no trousers' is the favourite phrase.

She tosses some shiny sheets of graphs and figures on to a table / desk. **Eddie** *picks them up, casually glances at them.* **Asha** *finally clocks* **Simon**.

Asha (*to* **Eddie**)   Who's this?

Simon (*jumps up, seizes her hand, shakes it*)   Hi, Simon Shadwick. Really pleased to be on board.

Asha (*withdrawing her hand*)   Oh, are you the gags bloke?

Simon   That's me.

Asha   You weren't meant to come straight up.

Simon   Oh, sorry. My mistake. Too eager by half, eh?

Asha   You need to liaise with Paul. He's not here. Wait downstairs, will you?

Simon   Yes, sure. That's cool. Call me when you need me. (*Heads for door.*)

Eddie   Stay where you are!

Simon   Oh. Right. Sorry.

Asha   He can wait downstairs, Eddie.

Eddie   He stays here, okay? He stays here.

Simon   Whatever . . . whatever's no trouble for you. (*Sits down again.*)

Eddie *casually throws down the focus group reports.*

Asha   Really worrying, aren't they?

Eddie   Yeah, well, compared to what, I suppose you might say.

Asha   You look terrible, George.

George (*to* **Asha**)   Actually, we have a little bit of a problem on our hands, Asha.

Asha   What kind of a problem?

Paul *enters, with a defiant air.*

Paul   No, Eddie, I haven't got the dirt on the idiots who jumped the platform. Because I've decided I respect them more than I respect you.

Eddie   Good decision. Couldn't agree more. Now. Get hold of the landlord of George's local, will you? George'll give you the number. (*Looks at* **George** *fumbling with papers.*) One day soon.

Asha   What kind of a problem?

Paul *puts hand in pocket, hands* **Eddie** *little plastic jar.*

Paul   Got you your vit C.

Eddie   Thanks.

Paul *picks up the cordless, goes over to* **George**, *confers, dials Directory Enquiries, gets number, dials it.*

Paul   Had to pay for it though. They'd never heard of you.

Eddie   That call. It's urgent.

Paul   Okay, okay.

Asha   What's going on, Eddie? (*Glances at a crumpled* **George**.)

Eddie   Yeah, well, how long have you got?

Asha   It's not the secret crop trials on George's land, is it?

Eddie   Oh, not you as well. Let's just issue a fucking press release, shall we? 'Ten things every member of the public needs to know about our secret crop trials.'

Asha   DL told me.

Eddie   Oh great. Anything else he's told you? Colour of his underwear?

George   She doesn't know about the breasts, Eddie.

Eddie *puts his head in his hands.*

Paul (*hands over cordless*)   Lamb and Flag. Landlord of. What breasts?

Eddie (*into cordless*)   Yeah. Hi. Look, I wonder if you can help me . . .

Eddie *turns upstage, heads away from the others, so we don't get to hear much of the call.*

Asha   Where do breasts come into crop trials?

Simon *thrusts himself forward, self-important.*

Simon   Well, apparently it's to do with the beer. You see, they've created this new strain of hops . . .

Paul (*to* **Simon**)   Who are you?

Simon   Simon Shadwick.

Paul   Oh Christ.

Asha   I told him to wait downstairs, Paul, but then –

Simon   Oh, you're Paul! Great. I gather we're teaming up on this one, Paul. Now do you want to give me the draft speech, and I'll funny it up? Or shall I give you a few gags I've been working on and you drop them in where appropriate? Or would it be better if we sat down together and –

Paul   Why don't you wait downstairs, Simon. You got a mobile?

Simon   No. There's some evidence they cause brain damage. Final proof came through last week when it was revealed that the leader of the opposition –

Paul   I'll lend you mine, and soon as I need you, I'll call you.

Eddie (*covering cordless mouthpiece*)   Paul. We know where all the media are staying, don't we?

Paul   Yes. It's on the data base.

Eddie   Find Liz for me. Find which hotel she's in.

Paul   What's this, a reconciliation?

Eddie (*shouts*)   Just do it!

Simon (*to* **Paul**)   I've already got some ideas for topicals. I work well under pressure, so if you want me to throw in a last-minute topical say tomorrow morning, then I –

Paul   Anyone seen my mobile?

Eddie   No.

Paul   Tell you what, Simon, just wait outside in the corridor.

Simon   Okay. Fine. No problem.

Simon *gets to the door.*

Eddie   Where do you think you're going?

Simon   I was just, you know . . . Sorry.

Eddie (*to* **Paul**)   He doesn't leave this room, got that?!

Paul (*shrugs. To* **Simon**, *indicating recliner*)   Okay. Why don't you sit down here instead? Relax, put your feet up.

Asha   Breasts. Secret crop trials. The connection. Anyone willing to help?

Paul *nudges* **Simon** *towards the recliner.* **Simon**, *bewildered, sits down on it, then lies out.*

Eddie (*into cordless*)   Thanks. Thanks. Great . . . Yeah. Bye. (*Switches cordless off. To* **Paul**.) Hurry it up, will you?

Paul *goes over to his laptop, taps on the keyboard, watches the screen.*

George   Is that Liz, as in your ex-missus?

Eddie   Yes.

George   Are you thinking she was the female journo in question?

Eddie   It's possible. The woman seen at your local answers her description. Sort of. Your brain-damaged landlord doesn't remember much.

George   If it is her, and if she's on to the story, can you talk her out of it?

To talk to **George**, **Eddie** *sits down on the edge of the recliner.* **Simon** *moves a leg out of the way.*

Eddie (*stares at* **George** *in silence for a moment*)   You haven't met Liz, have you?

George   No. Is she likely to be difficult?

Eddie   We didn't have a very friendly break-up.

George   Who does? (*Thinks.*) You really think it's Liz then, do you?

Eddie (*stands up*)   No. Paul's right, I just want us to get together again.

George (*missing the irony*)   Oh really?

Eddie (*shouts*)   No, not really, you fucking moron!

Asha   For God's sake, Eddie!

George   There's no need to be abusive.

Eddie (*struggling to be slow, calm and clear*)   George. You have helped organise compulsory gender realignment for God knows what percentage of the electorate, a situation which, if it's traced to us, is likely to make us unelectable for about a century and a half. (*Very loud.*) If I can't be abusive about that, what the fuck can I be abusive about?!

There is a pause. **Paul** *stares over at him.* **Asha** *frowns.*

Asha   Could you run that past me again?

Simon   He might want to make a clean breast of it. Ha!

Eddie   If you open your mouth one more time without being asked, I'll personally push you off the fucking balcony. (*Finally realises* **Simon** *is on his recliner.*) And don't sit there!

Simon (*leaps up*)   No. Of course not. Sorry.

Asha   What's going on?

Paul   Eddie. She's in the hotel.

Eddie   In what hotel?

Paul   Same one as we're in.

There's a moment's silence.

Eddie   That is weird.

Simon   This female journalist . . .

Eddie   Her rag can't afford this hotel.

Simon   This female journalist . . .

Eddie   Find her room number. Find her e-mail address. Find that computer geek who helped us with the Freedom of Information Bill. And make it quick.

Simon   This female journalist . . . Are you sure it isn't a male journalist who's just had too much of your beer? Ah-ha! Ah-ha! Ah-ha!

Everyone turns round to stare malevolently at **Simon**. **Simon**'*s laughter at his own joke slowly drains away.*

Sorry.

Blackout.

Music sting.

Act Two

Scene One

A room in the same hotel. The overall style is similar to that of the suite, but this room is humbler.

There is a double bed, a dressing table, a couple of soft chairs, a modest desk. There are lots of papers, files and clothes scattered around, jacket over the back of a chair, a towel on the floor. Open on the desk is a laptop or electronic notebook (switched on). Beside the laptop there are piles of papers, cards, notes. In front of the desk is a chair. On the dressing table there is an ashtray with several cigarette ends in it. Upstage left is the door through to the bathroom. Upstage centre is the door to the hotel corridor. On a hook on the back of the door hangs a clutter of clothes. Centre right is a window overlooking a back street.

When the curtain rises there is nobody in the room. On a small table by the bed is a speakerphone, with a red light glowing to show it is currently being used. From the bathroom we hear very faintly the sound of a shower.

Music. The music cross-fades into banal muzak from the speakerphone. We hear this for a few seconds. Then we hear a pre-recorded voice.

Recorded Voice 1 (*female*)   All our staff are busy at the moment. Your call is in a queue and will be answered as soon as possible. (*Music.*) All our staff are busy at the moment. Your call is in a queue and will be answered as soon as possible. (*Music.*)

The sound of the shower stops.

Recorded Voice 1   All our staff are busy at the moment. But your call has now been given a higher priority, and will be answered very shortly. (*Music.*)

The bathroom door opens and **Liz**'s *head appears, wrapped in a towel. She stares at the phone, listens.*

Recorded Voice 1   All our staff are busy at the moment. But your call has now been given a higher priority, and will be answered very shortly. (*Music.*)

Liz   Shit. (*Disappears back inside bathroom.*)

Recorded Voice 1   We apologise for the extended delay in responding to your call. This is caused by the fact that all our staff are busy due to the large number of callers presently calling. (*Music.*)

Liz *again appears at the bathroom door, stares at the speakerphone.*

Recorded Voice 1   You will shortly be connected to one of our friendly and helpful staff. Thank you for your patience. (*Music.*)

Liz   You're welcome.

Recorded Voice 2 (*male*)   Hello. You are through to the automated helpline for guests of the Belvedere Grand Hotel. To enable us to assist you with your enquiry, please press one for yes and two for no, or answer 'yes' or 'no' after the tone. Do you wish to order morning newspapers? (*Bleep.*)

Liz (*mutters*)   Oh for God's sake . . . (*Shouts.*) No!

She disappears into the bathroom again, leaving the door open.

Recorded Voice 2   Do you require information about hotel laundry services? (*Bleep.*)

Liz (*off*)   No!

Recorded Voice 2   I'm sorry. I didn't understand your reply. Do you require information about hotel laundry services? (*Bleep.*)

Liz (*appearing, shouts*)   No!!

Recorded Voice 2   Do you wish to have information about our leisure centre? (*Bleep.*)

Liz *comes close to the phone, shouts at it.*

Liz   No!

She goes over to dressing table, picks up pack of cigarettes.

Recorded Voice 2   Thank you. Our leisure centre is open to hotel residents from 7.30 a.m. till 9.30 p.m.

Liz's *shoulders buckle. She lights her cigarette.*

Recorded Voice 2   There is no charge for the use of the gymnasium, solarium or swimming pool, but a nominal charge of eighty pence per towel will be made for the provision of towels. Do you require information about other hotel services? (*Bleep.*)

Liz   Yes!

Recorded Voice 2   Do you require information about reservations for meals in the Wellington Suite? (*Bleep.*)

Liz   No!

Recorded Voice 2   Do you require information about reservations for meals in the Blenheim Room? (*Bleep.*)

Liz   No!

Recorded Voice 2   Do you wish to order food or refreshments from room service? (*Bleep.*)

Liz (*with exhausted triumphalism*)   Yes!!!

Recorded Voice 2   Thank you. Please hold while we connect you to room service. (*Music.*)

She goes to her laptop and logs on. We hear the faint sound of a computer dial-up.

Recorded Voice 3   Welcome to room service. Due to unusually high demand, all our room service operatives are currently busy. You call is in a queue and will be answered as soon as possible.

Liz   God almighty!

A synthesised computer voice is heard.

Synth (*female*)   You have new mail.

Recorded Voice 3   Welcome to room service. Due to unusually high demand, all our room service operatives are currently busy. Your call is in a queue and will be answered as soon as possible.

Her mobile rings. She can't find it. It's clear she's desperate not to miss the call. She scrabbles round in the mess of the bedroom, trying to detect the mobile by its sound.

Synth   You have new mail.

Recorded Voice 3   Welcome to room service. Due to exceptionally high demand, all our room service operatives are currently busy. Your call is in a queue and will be answered as soon as possible.

Synth   You have new mail.

Liz (*searching*)   Shit! . . . oh damn it . . . (*Finds it. Then into her mobile:*) Yes? . . . yes, speaking . . . You've got them?! Great! That's fantastic. Can you e-mail them to me? . . . Yes, that would be fine . . . Could you do it sooner than that? . . . Tremendous. Thanks. I'll be looking out for it . . . Thanks a lot. Thanks. (*Ends call.*)

Liz *goes to her laptop, taps a few keys, checks her e-mails.*

Recorded Voice 3   Welcome to room service. Due to exceptionally high demand, all our room service operatives are currently busy. Your call is in a queue and will be answered as soon as possible. Welcome to room service. Due to exceptionally high –

Waiter (*on speakerphone, breaking into recorded message*)   Hello. Thank you for calling room service. Barry speaking. How may I help you? Hello? . . . Hello?!

Liz (*rushes over towards speakerphone*)   Barry! I love you! Don't go away! (*Picks up phone, so that we don't hear the speaker any more – or maybe we hear a distant indication of his voice.*) Barry, where's the order for Room 735? . . . (*Struggling to stay calm.*) The order I put in about an hour and half ago, Barry . . . Yes, I did . . . I promise you, I did, Barry . . . (*Sighs.*) Seven-three-five . . . What? . . . Well, don't *you* have a note of what I ordered? . . . (*Resigned.*) Hold on. (*Phone still in hand, she rummages among the papers on the floor, finds the folder containing the hotel menu, opens it, picks up phone, reads seamlessly.*) . . . 'One triple-decker chicken, turkey and smoked ham club sandwich on oven-fresh granary bread with sliced avocado and crunchy bacon bits on a bed of crisp fresh salad smothered in our delicious creamy home-made mayonnaise. (*Beat.*) Garnished with crisps.' . . . Hold on, don't go away, Barry. I also ordered a bottle of (*pronounced correctly*) Rioja . . . Rioja . . . It's a wine, Barry . . . Rioja . . . (*Almost losing it now, pronounces it as if an English word.*) Ree. Odge. Ah . . . Thank you so much, Barry. (*Puts phone down, lets out shout of desperation.*) Aaaarrrrggghh!

She throws the menu on the bed, in frustration. She heads back towards the bathroom. There is a knock on the door. She gets up. She looks at the door, looks at the phone, looks back at the door, shakes her head, opens the door. **Eddie** *walks in. As he enters, he is checking the display on his mobile phone.*

Eddie   Hi, Liz. How's it going?

Liz   Eddie . . .

Eddie   Mind if I come in?

Liz   I think you're in.

Eddie (*puts phone away*)   Close the door then.

Liz   Why?

Eddie   I'd like to talk to you.

Liz   Why?

Eddie   Lighten up, Liz.

Liz   I'm not really dressed for visitors.

Eddie   That's all right, I'm not really a visitor.

She closes the door. **Eddie***'s eyes go to the laptop and the desk (though the laptop screen can't be seen by him).* **Liz** *moves to the desk, clicks* *the mouse a couple of times. She tidies notes away, maybe drops a newspaper over some of them, the aim being to conceal them from* **Eddie**.

Liz   Bit of a mess here.

Eddie   Never bothered you before. Let me help.

He reaches for a document; she snatches it away. There is a moment of silence as they look at each other. **Liz** *lights a cigarette and rather deliberately blows out the smoke.* **Eddie** *coughs slightly, waves the smoke away.*

How about offering me a drink?

Liz   You'll only want a fucking mineral water.

Eddie   Might not. Try me.

Liz   Would you like a drink, Eddie?

Eddie   Thanks. I'll have fucking mineral water.

He grins. She doesn't. She goes to the minibar, rummages. She hands him a small bottle of mineral water, without a glass, and gets a miniature of vodka for herself, pours it into a glass.

Liz   Sorry. Only got one glass. This end of the hotel's a bit iffy. I think they've diverted all the staff to your end. Took me about an hour to get through to room service.

Eddie   I can give you our special number, if you like. Goes straight through to the kitchens.

Liz   No thanks.

He opens the bottle of water, waves away the smoke, looks round the messy room.

Eddie   No big lifestyle changes, I see.

Liz   No. Should I have big lifestyle changes?

Eddie   Might help you live longer, I suppose.

Liz   Might. Might not. That's the thing about life, isn't it? You never quite know when it'll end. Even vegetarians have that problem. You still a vegetarian, Eddie?

Eddie   Yes.

Liz   Oh good. I'm so happy for you and the vegetables. I presume you want something?

Eddie   A chat.

Liz   A chat?

Eddie   Yes.

Liz   Middle of Conference week?

Eddie   Yes.

Liz   Day before Diddums has to make his big speech?

Eddie   Yes.

Liz   Ooo-er. Very mysterious. And you've left Diddums all on his own? I trust he's coping.

Eddie (*smiles*)   Yeah, just about. How's life on *Red Bollocks*, then? Anyone still reading that thing?

Liz   Yes, in fact, *Red Rostrum* is doing quite well.

Eddie   Surprised they can afford to let you stay in this place. (*Waves vaguely to indicate the hotel.*) Paying for it yourself?

Liz (*caught off guard*)   Might be.

Eddie   Ah. I see. So you're spending several hundred quid for a few nights in the deeply tacky Belvedere Grand . . . weird.

Liz   I felt like being close to the action.

Eddie   Depends where the action is. I gather you've been hanging around George Warmley's estate.

Liz   George Warmley's estate? Don't even know where it is.

Eddie   Would you like some help with that story?

Liz   What story's that?

Eddie   I could let you have a few interesting details.

Liz   Why would you want to do that?

Eddie   Poor old George, he's past his sell-by date, really. If some bad publicity forced him to resign, well, how can I put it? I think I'd cope with the grievous sense of loss.

Liz   God, it's ferrets in a sack, isn't it? What do you do for relaxation, push each other out of aeroplanes?

Eddie   So you're not interested in a story that could bring down a Cabinet minister?

Liz   Well, I'm not against it in principle. If there is such a story.

Eddie   I think you know there is.

Liz   When did you develop these mind-reading skills?

Eddie   This is a bit odd, isn't it?

Liz   Is it?

Eddie   Yes, Liz, it's fucking, amazingly, stupendously odd. Here's a minister we all despise, here's a chance to send him to the rubbish bin, here's a story that'll put your name on the front pages again. And you don't seem very interested.

Liz   I've lost my touch. Remember?

Eddie   Maybe you've got a bigger story.

Liz   That would be lovely, of course.

Eddie *considers his next move.*

Eddie   Liz. I know it was you down on George's estate.

Liz   I don't think you do.

Eddie*'s mobile rings. He checks the caller display, then answers it. He moves away from* **Liz**.

Eddie   Yep? . . . Good. And what's it come up with?
(*Takes out pen and card, makes notes.*) . . . Right . . . Right . . .
How often? . . . Got it . . . Oh really? How many? . . . Sixty-
two? Great. Any others? . . . Yes, could be . . . Anything else
I should know? . . . Right . . . Oh. Oh yes . . . Oh that's fun.
I'll have that . . . Yes . . . No, that'll be enough for now.
Thanks for this. Bye. (*Switches off. He stares at his notes for a
moment.*) Tell me, Liz. Ever taken a look at George
Warmley's business interests?

Liz   Not that I recall.

Eddie   It's on the Net. Register of Interests for the House
of Lords. Ever so easy to access.

Liz   So what?

Eddie   Well, you see, I've just been informed you hit that
website twice in the last week. And both those hits were in
the section for members beginning with 'W'. So whose
interests were you checking other than Warmley's?

Liz   I can't remember. Wankers? What is this?

Eddie (*looks at notes again*)   You also visited the Progenitor
website rather a lot. As well as sixty-two other websites
dealing with GM crops. Fascinating, eh? (*Referring to notes.*)
Are you thinking of taking up home-brewing? You seem to
be very interested in hops. Funny, I don't remember you as
a beer drinker. Oh, and a poignant detail here . . .
Apparently last Thursday night you checked out a site called
Luxury Weekend Breaks for the Discerning Single
Traveller. Bit sad that, isn't it?

Liz   Piss off.

Eddie   Expecting a windfall, are you? Sudden leap in
earnings, perhaps? (*Puts notes away.*) Not that *Red Bollocks* is
going to pay you much. What's the plan, sell the story on to
the *Sunday Times*? Or the *Mail* perhaps. Nice people at the
Mail, very cuddly.

Liz   I don't know how you managed this, Eddie, but –

Eddie   It's surprisingly easy, and quick. And unlike phone taps, you don't need a warrant.

Liz   You are such a bunch of shits.

Eddie   Did you by any chance get an e-mail earlier, from an outfit called cheapcigarettesdotcom? Half-price cigarettes, all entirely legal?

Liz   Yes . . . You mean . . . that came from you?

Eddie   I told them you wouldn't be able to resist.

Liz   I don't get it.

Eddie   Well, when you downloaded it, you activated a very clever little programme. It's so clever, it gathers up your entire Internet history from your hard drive. And e-mails it on to a friend of mine. Who just called me. (*Indicates his mobile.*)

Liz   Aren't you the people who believed in freedom of information?

Eddie   Yeah. Our freedom, your information.

Liz   Are you proud? Nastier than the KGB. More efficient than the CIA. That was in the manifesto, was it?

Eddie   Hey . . . manifesto . . . So?

Liz (*takes it in for a moment*)   Of course, I'm not sure it helps you a great deal. Because you don't know how much I know. Which is a bit of a problem for you, isn't it?

Eddie   You're waiting for something, there's a piece of the story missing, am I right?

Liz   No.

Eddie   I think I'm right.

Liz   You always thought that. It's a guy thing.

Eddie   If you've got everything you need, why haven't you published?

Liz   Well, maybe I'm just taking my time about it.

Eddie   No. You're jumpy. You're tense. You're drinking.

Liz   It's your electric presence, Eddie. Any chance of taking it some place else?

The hotel phone rings. **Eddie** *snatches it up.*

Eddie   Yeah? No granary bread? . . . who is this? Forget it, Barry.

Liz   No!

Eddie   Yeah. Cancel it. We're busy.

Liz   Aargh! Have you any idea how long it took me to –?

There is a 'ping' from the laptop. **Liz** *hurries over, excited.*

Synth   You have new mail.

Eddie   Ah.

Liz, *about to download, suddenly stops.*

Liz   If I open this . . . will you end up . . . you know . . . getting hold of it?

Eddie   Oh, I'm afraid a copy will already be on its way to us. Sorry about that.

Liz   Well, fuck it. (*She clicks and downloads.*)

Eddie   There's my girl.

Liz (*reads the e-mail on screen*)   Oh yes . . . Oh very good . . . Oh yes.

Eddie   Let me see it. Might as well. Save me the price of a phone call.

Liz   No.

Eddie   Let me see it.

Liz   No. No. I want to read it to you. I'd really like to read it to you. It's the results of a series of tests. (*Reads.*) 'The beer made from the genetically modified hops was fed to a total of one hundred male laboratory rats over a thirty-day period. The dosage was calculated at . . . blah blah . . . equivalent to a daily consumption of just under four pints for an adult male human . . . et cetera . . . At the end of the trial period, eighty-two of the rats showed clear signs of feminisation, with some indications of genital shrinkage and marked growth of mammary tissue.' That's it. Interesting, eh? So . . . if you'll excuse me, I have a story to file.

Eddie's *mobile rings. He answers it.*

Eddie   Yeah? . . . What, the lab report? . . . Forget it, I know already . . . I said forget it . . . what? . . . because she just fucking read it to me, okay? (*He rings off.*) . . . God . . .

Eddie *sits down heavily on the edge of the bed.* **Liz** *looks at him, lights another cigarette, pours herself another drink, moves around a bit.*

Liz   Cheer up. It's not all bad, you know. Men with tits. It's a unique achievement for a political party. Puts everything else in the shade, wouldn't you say? Men with tits, that's what I call a radical reform. Has the Prime Minister had some of your dodgy beer, do you think? Might be good if he has. He can lead by example. Think how the nation would be inspired by a bit of breastfeeding on the steps of Number Ten. Now there's a photo-opportunity to die for. You'd have to get the Murdoch press onside first, of course. It might take *Sun* readers a little time to get used to Page Three hermaphrodites, don't you think? Maybe the Prime Minister could be the first. 'The pouting PM–38, 34, six inches – says he wants his breasts to be a beacon to the world. Cor, say we, who wouldn't want to be guided to them two beacons on a dark night! They're a *shining* example of what makes Britain a great place to live! Har har har!' Then of course it would be good material for putting the frighteners on all those teachers and doctors and civil servants who're clinging to outmoded ideas about where bosoms belong. Yes, that's definitely the way to spin this, Eddie. Go on the offensive, seize the high ground, turn defeat into opportunity, send DL out to make speeches with that mad Messianic glint in his eye. Speeches. Great speeches. With. Many. Short. Sentences. Pithy. Pointed. Honest. New horizons. Vision. Change. Adapting to change. Men – yes. Women – yes. But now, the Third Way: men and women. Together. In one body. The way of the future. Here. Now. A new Britain. We can do it. Together. With your enthusiasm. Your energy. Your commitment. And . . . your . . . boobs. Thank you. (*Flops down on the bed, looks up, then casually:*) So, what do you think?

Eddie   You're really going to publish this?

Liz   Oh, for Christ's sake. Eddie. It's the best story I'm ever going to have in my life. You think I'm going to pass it up?

Eddie   This isn't going to be one of your worthy little pieces about asylum seekers, you know. This is going to be so big.

Liz   I'm ready for that.

Eddie   You sure?

Liz   I'll cope.

Eddie   You didn't before.

Liz   We're talking a long time ago.

Eddie   People have long memories.

Liz   It was just depression. I survived.

Eddie   Only because I got you treatment. Sorry. It's true. I'm just concerned it could happen again, Liz. Look what happened when you were riding high before. Your own newspaper column twice a week. And a very good one too. Used to scare them at Westminster. And what did you do? You hit the bottle. You hit drugs. And you hit the editor.

Liz   That wasn't my best career move. Enjoyed it, though.

Eddie   You were regularly too drunk to deliver your copy on time. And you fucked up on that book you were meant to write.

Liz   Yeah, okay, but I can handle the drink now.

Eddie   Oh yes?

She deliberately pours another drink.

Liz   You know something, Eddie, when you drank, you were a nicer man.

Eddie   I was ugly. Drunks are ugly.

Liz   Yes, but at least you were a human being – ugly, drunk, but more or less a recognisable human being. You know? With ideals, and stuff like that?

Eddie   I'm not full of romantic bullshit any more, if that's what you mean. Emotionally, you're still stuck somewhere back in the time of the miners' strike.

Liz   Oh, is that so?

Eddie   Yeah. It's never been so good again, has it? The miners' strike, life and death for some. But for you, just a big girl's adventure story. Liz and Eddie driving up to Yorkshire by night to hand over food parcels. Liz and Eddie evading the police road blocks. Liz spending the night having D.H. Lawrence fantasies about horny-handed sons of toil bringing her to orgasm.

Liz   Those weren't just fantasies.

Eddie   Aw Christ . . .

Liz   That second trip. The big jolly bloke who –

Eddie   I don't want to know, I don't want to know.

Liz   They laughed at you. When you weren't around, they laughed at you.

Eddie   Yeah, well, they were a bunch of losers. Led by a demagogue, and supported by a sad little band of middle-class romantics. People like you.

Liz   I was twenty-three for Christ's sake! If you can't get a little bit romantic about changing the world then, when can you?

Eddie   Some of us have moved on.

Liz   At least I still believe in something. What do you believe in now, Eddie?

Eddie   Aw, don't give me the self-righteous crap. You think you're the only one who believes in anything?

Liz   Okay. What exactly is it you've achieved?

Eddie   I helped make the party credible. I helped make it electable.

Liz   Oh, I know you're good at getting elected. But what about after? How about a bit of radical change? How about redistribution of wealth? That's not on the agenda, is it? That would upset the rich. You don't believe in doing that. That would mean conflict. That would mean real politics. And you want to take the politics out of politics.

Eddie   No, we want to get beyond the old politics of left and right.

Liz   Oh, come on, you know where all that consensual bollocks takes you. You end up trying to govern without choosing. Which can't really be done. So all you end up with is presentation. Government by headline. Making people feel good. It's the feelgood factor. It's all you care about.

Eddie   You can't achieve anything unless you get people onside.

Liz   You can't have everyone onside! If that's your aim, you'll just keep on tinkering around the edges.

Eddie   It's called incremental change.

Liz   But nothing's really getting any better! Christ, have you been on a train recently, have you tried getting a hospital appointment?

Eddie   It takes time to change things.

Liz   You don't have time! People are getting hacked off.

Eddie   They still vote for us, though, don't they?

Liz   Well, people are going to have to be very desperate to want the other lot, aren't they? But underneath it all, they're getting hacked off with politics. Because it doesn't seem to change anything much. They'll end up not caring who's in power. Which is why you lot aren't just going to fuck the party. You're going to fuck democracy.

Eddie   I see. Anything else we're going to fuck?

Liz   Yeah, but that'll do to be going on with.

Eddie   It's us or the other lot, Liz. And you know we're still better news than the other lot. What a bunch: xenophobic, racist, bigoted, nasty, unprincipled, opportunistic. Basically, shits.

Liz   I'm not asking anyone to vote for them.

Eddie   Yes, you fucking well are! That's exactly what you're doing. If you run a story that could bring down the government, effectively you're asking people to vote in the other lot.

Liz   That's . . . look, it's not my job to think about that.

Eddie   Oh, really? Quite sure? (*Goes over to* **Liz**, *puts a hand on her arm.*) Put the story on hold, Liz. For six months. We can rethink the whole GM strategy. If you wanted to write a briefing paper on it, I'd put it in front of DL. You can meet him.

Liz   Ooo-er. Little me allowed inside Diddums' Big Tent.

Eddie   There are probably other issues you could help us on. You'd be changing things from within.

Liz (*sceptical*)   Are you trying to tell me Diddums is going to listen to me?

Eddie   Yes. If I tell him to. I wish you wouldn't call him Diddums.

Liz   These other issues . . . what kind of issues?

Eddie   Anything. Immigration. Asylum.

Liz   I see . . .

Eddie   His intincts are radical, Liz. Only he's surrounded by second-raters. (*Grins.*) Apart from me of course. He recognises talent. He'd recognise yours. He respects people who can argue their corner well. His door would be open for you. I'd make sure of that. Don't you like the idea of being at the centre of things?

Liz   After I publish this story, believe me, I'll be at the centre of things.

Eddie   No, no, no. Journalists are always on the outside. Even successful ones. They think they're on the inside, but they're not. No, I mean, in close. In where you can actually achieve something. That's where you could be, Liz. Right in there with power. In bed with it. It's a fucking wonderful feeling, Liz.

Liz   Oh my God, Eddie. It's got you by the bollocks. Like it gets them all.

Eddie   Okay. Maybe it has. So what. Power means you get things done. That's what it's for.

She crosses to the minibar, opens it.

You want to get things done, Liz. Don't you?

She takes out a bottle of beer, turns.

Liz   Sorry, I'm out of mineral water. (*She holds up a bottle of beer.*) You don't fancy a beer, by any chance, do you?

Blackout.

Music: R. Kelly's 'I Believe I Can Fly' fills the auditorium, continues during the scene change, and over the first twenty seconds or so of the next scene.

Scene Two

Two to three hours later. It's now early evening.

Lights up on the wonks' suite (same as Act One). The song continues, and turns into music coming from a CD player on stage. A distraught **Eddie** *is pacing up and down in front of the doors that lead to the PM's rooms.* **George** *is near him, his attention also on the PM's door.* **George** *has a glass of white wine in one hand, which he replenishes from a half-empty bottle of Pinot Grigio. Every now and then* **George** *gets in the way of* **Eddie**'s *impatient pacing.* **Paul** *is at his keyboard, staring in the direction of the PM's door.* **Simon** *is at 'his' desk, a bit forlorn.* **Asha** *is by the CD player, listening to the music. There is a pile of CD boxes beside her. The song has almost ended.* **Asha** *switches it off.*

Asha   That's the one. That's definitely the one. Okay. Speech finishes. Cue music. DL waves, takes the applause, comes down from the platform, makes his way out through the auditorium, pressing the flesh as he goes. Another Conference triumph. (*Looks round at everybody.*) Can I get some feedback here, please!

There is silence. Everybody else is focused on **DL**'s *door.* **Eddie** *takes out a pill from a foil pack, swigs from his bottle of water.*

Eddie (*to* **George**)   I never thought it would take this long.

George   Neither did I.

Eddie   God.

Eddie *puts his ear to the PM's doors, holds up a hand.*

George (*to* **Eddie**)   Hear anything?

Eddie   Shhh!

Asha   Listen, Eddie. You said it would take fifteen minutes and she's been in with DL for nearly an hour and a half now. Is she going to publish, or is she not?

Eddie (*gives up on listening at door*)   I don't know, do I? She's obviously being difficult. Is that meant to be my fault? (*Rubs forehead in pain.*) Christ. (*Tears open another foil pack of pills.*)

George   Headaches always come at the wrong moment, don't they?

Eddie   It's not a headache, George. I didn't say headache. Did I say headache? It's a migraine, George.

George (*to* **Eddie**)   Yes. Right. Migraine. Absolutely. (*To* **Asha**.) There's a lot hanging on this, Asha.

Eddie   There's everything hanging on this.

Asha   Yes, but we can't just put everything else on hold. Paul ought to be getting on with DL's speech.

Paul   Which speech is that, Asha? The one where he does a broad-ranging review of the government's achievements, the one where he sets our pulses racing with his vision of a crime-free future, or the one where he breaks the bad news to beer drinkers?

Simon   Um, would you like me to work up some gags for each of those options?

Asha, **Eddie**, **Paul**   No!

Simon   Sorry. The ball's in your court. I'm here when you need me.

Asha (*to* **Paul**)   Whether Liz comes on board or not, DL's still got to make the speech tomorrow, right? It's nearly eight now, he'll want to rehearse it on autocue by midnight, so can you please keep going?

Paul   Okay, okay. Hey, just think, I could be writing his last major speech as Prime Minister.

George   Oh, dear God.

Asha   How could you say that?

Eddie   I don't want to hear that, okay, I don't want to hear that.

Paul   Did I say something wrong?

George *wanders over to the CD pile, casually picks up a couple of CD boxes, looks at them. With a glance in the direction of the PM's door,* **Eddie** *crosses to* **Paul**.

Eddie   All right, sorry. Let's try to get this thing wrapped.

Asha   Thank you. At last.

Eddie (*stops as a thought hits him*)   They don't have alcohol in there, do they?

Asha   No.

George   I think we'll probably be all right, Eddie.

Eddie   Probably? Probably? How's that work exactly, 'probably'?

George   All I mean is, DL's tremendously persuasive, and let's not forget that. You've done a fantastic job getting them together like this, Eddie. The rest is up to DL. And he's brilliant at getting people onside. You weren't there when he charmed the socks off that Vladimir Putin fellow. Young Vlad really worships DL now.

Paul   Must be nice to be worshipped by a murdering thug.

George   Why do you have to spoil everything, Paul, with your . . . your . . politics! You know, I'm very much inclined to have a word with DL about you. There's plenty other young smart-asses around we could hire in your place. (*To*

Asha, *waving CD box.*) This 'pop song' of yours, Asha . . . 'I Believe I Can Fly' . . . It's not very . . . prime ministerial, is it?

Asha   It's aspirational, George. It's saying to ordinary people, trust in your dreams. Trust in us and you can be anything you want to be.

Paul   Yeah, you can even be a man with tits.

Eddie *puts his head in his hands for a moment, then his attention goes back to PM's door.*

Eddie   Asha, you could go in with more coffee. Report back on the atmosphere in there. Is that a good idea? Oh God, I don't know, maybe that'll just blow it. Let's wait. Let's wait some more. How long should we wait?

Asha   I think the best thing we can do for DL is get everything ready for tomorrow.

Simon   Excuse me, I've been wondering . . . this is a bit embarrassing, because really, I ought to know, but why do you call him DL? I mean, those aren't his real initials, are they?

George   DL. Divine Light. It's a sort of . . . affectionate send-up.

Simon   Divine Light. Oh yes, very good. Divine Light.

George   Reflects the tremendous faith we have in him, actually.

Paul   Alternative versions include Dodgy Leader and Dreadfully Lightweight.

Eddie (*looks over at PM's door, checks his watch*)   We'll give them five more minutes. Then you're going in there, Asha. Or should it be me? No, can't be me. Liz would turn nasty, just on principle. Has to be you.

Asha   Eddie. The speech.

Eddie   Yes, sure. Okay. Paul. Where had we got to?

Paul   GM crops, I'm afraid. Option Two: GM might be good, might be bad, let's wait and see.

George   What about Jerusalem? That always goes down well. (*Sings.*) 'And did those feet in ancient times . . .'

Asha   I don't actually think we can suggest he's the son of God, do you?

Simon   Though turning water into wine would definitely be worth a few points in the polls, eh? Not to mention the feeding of the five thousand.

Eddie (*spins round, stares at* **Simon**)   That's good! That's very good.

Simon (*surprised*)   Oh. Thank you. It's not a gag as such. But I could tweak it a little.

Eddie   Yeah. Feeding of the five thousand . . . Take it from the GM crops.

Paul   Okay. (*Reads.*) 'So GM crops could transform the prospects of the world's poor.'

Eddie (*dictates as* **Paul** *types*)   A modern miracle. The feeding of the five thousand.

George   Oh, brilliant idea, Eddie. Very well done.

Eddie   No loaves . . .

Paul   No loaves . . .

Eddie   No fishes . . .

Paul   No fishes . . .

Eddie   Just this grain of rice.

Paul   Just this grain . . .

Eddie   We're going to need a grain of rice.

Paul   I'll pop down to Sainsbury's and get one right away.

Asha   It's good, Eddie.

Eddie   Thanks.

Simon *has picked up another phone, starts dialling.*

Eddie (*sharply to* **Simon**)   What are you doing?

Simon   Making a call.

Eddie *goes over, takes phone from him.*

Eddie   I'd rather you didn't.

Simon   Look, at some point you're going to have to let me make contact with the outside world. You do know you can trust me, don't you? I mean, nothing I've heard here will pass my lips.

Eddie (*putting an arm round his shoulder*)   This sitcom of yours, Simon. *Nobody's* . . . (*Waves his hand vaguely.*)

Simon   *Perfect. Nobody's Perfect.* (*Sings.*) 'Nobody's perfect, not on your life, Nobody's perfect, take a look at my wife.'

Eddie   Right. I'm sure you'd love to see it go to a second series, am I right?

Simon   Oh, well, I think it will, you know. It's the BBC's only successful comedy right now.

Eddie (*glancing in direction of PM's door*)   Which goes for nothing, Simon, if the DG takes against it. You might not even get any repeats.

Simon   He wouldn't stop the repeats, would he?

Eddie   Well, you never know. As it happens, I'm having lunch with him next week. He owes me one, so I'll mention it.

Simon   Oh that would be fantastic. Thanks.

Eddie   We look after our friends, you know, Simon. And in return . . .

Simon   Mum's the word.

Eddie   Good boy. (*Turns his attention back to the PM's door.*) Okay, Asha. Here's the plan. You go in there, quite casually . . .

Simon   Look. I really want to do my bit for tomorrow's speech. I've got a couple of ideas for funnies, thought I might run them by you.

Eddie   Later, okay?

Simon   Fine, fine, sure. I'll polish them a bit, then.

Eddie   Great. Asha –

Simon *goes over towards* **Eddie**.

Simon   I thought I might give DL this great gag about the Deputy Prime Minister. I saw him on the six o'clock news, you see, being driven away from a broken-down train. In a big Daimler. So I –

Paul   In a Daimler?

Simon   So I thought DL could say –

Asha   Not now, Simon!

Simon   Okay. Right. Sorry.

Eddie   Okay, Asha, here's the plan, you go in there quite casually, right?

Paul   How come he was in a Daimler? I told transport to send a small car.

George *empties the last of the white wine into his glass.* **Asha**'s *bleeper goes. She looks at it.*

Asha   It's DL . . .

Eddie   Yeah? What's happening?

Asha   He wants . . . he wants me to send in a round of drinks. (*Reads.*) Large vodka for Liz . . . and a glass of the usual for DL.

George   Oh God.

Asha *hurries over to the minibar, takes out key, opens it.*

Eddie   What?

George   His favourite Pinot Grigio. (*Holds up the bottle in his hand, turns it upside down to show it's empty.*) I'm afraid this was his last bottle.

Eddie   Oh great, George, very well done!

George   Well, he only brought one case with him this year! I'm very, very sorry. Mea culpa. Mea fucking culpa.

Asha, *fussing around in the fridge, pulls out a bottle of white.*

Asha   All we've got is a bottle of house white.

George   House white? We can't give him house white!

Asha   We'll have to.

The sound of police sirens is heard, and a crowd noise, louder than before. **George** *gets up, goes over to the big window.*

Asha *starts sorting out the drinks.*

George (*at balcony window*)   God almighty. Why are the police allowing them this near? I hope they know what they're doing.

Simon   Can I help?

Asha   Oh. Yes. All right. Open this bottle. (*She hands him bottle with corkscrew stuck in it.*)

Simon *helps organise the drinks on to a tray.*

George *opens the balcony doors, cautiously goes out. The noise of shouting, singing is clearly heard. Then the sound of breaking glass, followed by cheering.*

George (*half visible on balcony*)   Bloody hell! (*Something hits* **George** *in the face. He staggers backs with a cry of pain.*) Ahh! (*He staggers into the room, a hand over his face. His tone is panicky.*) I've been hit! God . . . a half brick or something . . . Oh my God . . . get a doctor . . .

Asha *rushes over to* **George**. **Paul** *also goes over.* **Eddie** *approaches, watches.* **Simon** *stares for a moment, then gets on with preparing the drinks.*

Asha   Let me see it, George, let me see . . .

Eddie *goes out on to the balcony.*

George   Is there . . . is there a lot of blood?

Asha (*looking*)   No. No sign of blood.

Eddie, *on balcony, picks something up.*

George   God, it hurts, it hit me just there . . . Something incredibily hard. Lot of bruising, is there?

Asha   No, but that eye looks a bit rough . . .

Simon, *unnoticed by the others, takes the tray, and cheerfully goes to the PM's door, knocks briefly, and goes in.* **Eddie** *comes back in, holding a potato.*

George   Oh God, is my eye injured? Things have gone too far when they can start hurling bricks and stones at our – (*Looks at* **Eddie**'s *hand.*) What's that?

Eddie   A baked potato.

George   Well, why on earth are you standing there with a – ?

Eddie   George. You were hit by a baked potato.

George   A baked potato?

Eddie   Yes. I think you'll live. (*Slaps the potato down on the table, turns his attention back to the PM's door.*)

George   Well . . . well, just because it was a baked potato doesn't mean it's not painful! Have you ever been hit by a baked potato, Eddie, eh, you tell me that! And it was probably a looted baked potato. They're smashing and burning down there, you know, God only knows what will happen if they get any closer.

Eddie   Shut up! (*Suddenly focused.*) Where's Simon?

Asha   Yes. Where's Simon?

They all clock the fact that **Simon**'s *gone.* **Asha** *looks at where the tray was.*

Paul (*pointing*)   He's in there . . .

There is a moment of horrified silence as they stare at the PM's door and absorb the information. They remain staring at the PM's door in silence for several seconds.

DL (*off*)   Ha ha ha ha ha.

Asha   It's DL.

Paul   Laughing.

DL (*off*)   Ha ha ha ha ha.

Simon (*off*)   Haaaaaaaaaa!

A moment later, the PM's door opens, and **Simon**, *empty tray in hand, comes out, closes door behind him.*

Simon   Haaaaaaaaaa! What a nice man.

Paul   Was he . . . did he . . . laugh at one of your jokes?

Simon   Yeah. Loved it. Apparently his kids would like to meet me. I'm invited to Chequers. (*To* **Asha**.) He says you'll sort out a date.

Eddie   Oh, Jesus . . .

Simon   You're very well thought of by DL, you know, Asha. He says you do absolutely everything for him.

Eddie   Yeah, I did wonder.

Simon   I think he meant things like sorting out his ties for him, actually.

Simon *goes off to a corner, gets his diary out.* **Asha** *glances at her watch.*

Asha   Oh damn. His suit. I haven't collected his suit for tomorrow. (*To* **Eddie**.) You and Paul will get on with the speech, won't you?

Eddie (*mimicking her*)   Yes, Asha. We will get on with the speech.

Asha *leaves.*

George   I . . . I need to eat something. Sorry. It's the stress.

Eddie   How about a baked potato, George, why don't you eat a fucking baked potato? (*He almost pushes the potato in* **George***'s face.*)

George   You want to watch it, Eddie. You're hysterical. I'm going down to the Blenheim Room for a steak.

Eddie   You do that. (*Takes out sealed envelope from jacket pocket.*) You might like to read this over supper.

George (*taking it*)   What is it?

Eddie   Your letter of resignation.

George   Eh?

Eddie   Just a precaution, George. In case you have to do the decent thing.

George   I'm not planning to do the decent thing, Eddie. I won't be scapegoated here.

Eddie   Look. The fucking stuff was on your land. If we need a scapegoat, I'm afraid you're the winning candidate.

George   Forget it. I care about this job. I passed up half a million quid a year in fees to do this job, Eddie. I like this job. I like being in government. I'm not resigning. Anyhow, I could bring DL down with me, if I wanted to.

Eddie   May I have a word in your ear, George?

Putting an arm around him, **Eddie** *leads* **George** *downstage left.*

Eddie   Late one night in November 1994? Behind King's Cross? In your car? You forgot about the CCTV cameras.

George *gulps, crumples.*

Eddie   Go and have your meal now, eh?

George   Yes . . . yes . . . that's an excellent idea. (*Crosses to door.*) Shan't be long.

Eddie   You can be as long as you like, George.

George *leaves.* **Simon** *looks up from his diary.*

Simon   I could do next weekend, but the one after's a bit tricky because – oh, where's she gone? You know, it's very difficult organising you people.

Eddie   Shhh!

Liz *has entered. They watch, frozen. She stops, stands still. She takes out a pack of cigarettes, fumbles with them a bit, and lights one. She blows out a long column of smoke.* **Eddie** *waits expectantly.*

Liz   I think he took against me at first.

Eddie   Why?

Liz   I forgot to curtsy.

She goes to the balcony, opens a door, peers out. The sound of riots and violence is clearly heard.

Liz   There's always someone else somewhere having more fun than you, isn't there? (*Turns back downstage.*) There appears to be a proper riot going on out there. Not a wispy, wimpy, half-hearted, British demo, but a real rollicking old-fashioned riot – with looting and burning! There's hope for this country after all. I only wish I had the guts to go and join in.

Eddie (*without taking his eyes off* **Liz**)   Paul. This is private.

Paul   Tough shit.

Eddie   Get out.

Paul No.

Eddie I said, get out.

Paul No.

Eddie Just fucking get out!

Paul No.

Liz, *half-amused, has followed the exchanges as if they were a ping-pong match.*

Liz What would you say was the secret of your working relationship? Mutual respect? Trust? Grace under pressure? A vigorous yet curiously dry sense of humour?

Simon I was quite struck by DL's sense of humour, you know. He seems to appreciate a well-honed gag.

Eddie (*having forgotten about him*) Oh Christ . . . Simon, you need to take a leak.

Simon Do I?

Eddie Yes.

Simon I thought you wanted me to polish my gags?

Eddie Yes. But if you could . . . you know, just for five minutes or so . . . Better make that a shit.

Simon But I don't need a shit.

Eddie Yes, you do.

Simon Oh, all right.

Simon *gets up, moves towards the door to the bathroom.*

Liz That's an awesome charisma you've got there, Eddie. You can make a grown man defecate. Just like that. (*Snaps her fingers.*)

Eddie (*to* **Simon**) Hang on. There's a better solution. (*To* **Liz**.) You and I'll go in there.

Simon Do I still need a shit?

Eddie   No, not any more. Thanks anyway.

Liz   It's okay, Eddie. I'm not publishing.

Eddie *stops in his tracks.*

Paul   Why not?

Eddie (*to* **Paul**)   Stay out! (*To* **Liz**.) You're definitely not publishing?

Liz   That's right.

She goes in her handbag, pulls out a floppy disk.

It's all on here. You'd better look after it. My hard disk seems to have developed a mysterious virus.

Eddie *takes the floppy, puts it in the pocket of his jacket, which is over the back of a chair.*

Eddie (*excited*)   This is great. This is wonderful. It's a good decision, Liz, a good decision. I won't forget this. DL won't forget it.

Liz   Don't worry, I got something in return.

Eddie   That's okay, that's cool, that's fine. What did you get in return?

Liz   He's agreed to put up income tax by ten pee in the pound.

Eddie   Eh!

Liz   And up by thirty pee for high earners.

Eddie   Liz . . .

Liz   All part of a massive redistribution of wealth. Starting with big increases in welfare spending. Pensions up by fifty per cent. Let me see . . .

Eddie   Liz . . .

Liz   No more road building. Massive subsidies for public transport. Renationalisation of the railways – without compensation. The directors of Railtrack to be reappointed as station cleaners. Now what else was there . . .

Eddie   Liz, stop messing around, there's no time.

Liz   Okay. You're going to repeal the Asylum Act.

Eddie   No, seriously . . .

Liz   Seriously. I promise you.

Eddie   We're going to repeal it? All if it? DL said that?

Liz   Yes. No more detention centres. No more vouchers. Just a bit of humanity at last.

Eddie   Fucking hell . . . Okay. Fine. The press won't like it, but fuck it. Yeah, repeal the Asylum Act. No sweat.

Liz   He's putting me in charge of a special commission.

Eddie   Great.

Liz   To oversee the drafting of a new framework for immigration and asylum.

Paul   That isn't going to do any good!

Eddie (*to* **Paul**)   I told you to stay out of this! (*To* **Liz**.) That's fantastic, Liz. (*He grabs her, whirls her round, tries to kiss her. She draws away.*) You're a star. Welcome aboard. We'll celebrate, you and me. After Conference. My invite.

Liz   I'll think about it.

Eddie   Look, I'd better . . . I mean, I ought to talk to DL . . .

Liz   Of course.

Eddie   Thanks. Thanks, Liz. Good decision. (*As he heads for the door through to the PM's room, he balls his fist hard.*) Yeah! (*Knocks on door, cautiously opens it.*) Prime Minister? . . . (*Leaves, closes door behind him.*)

Paul *gets up to go over to* **Liz**, *but is pipped to it by* **Simon**.

Paul   Listen, can we – ?

Simon (*to* **Liz**)   Hi. We weren't introduced properly in there. I'm Simon Shadwick. Comedy adviser to the Prime Minister.

Liz   Would you say it's a fun job?

Simon   It's not been a great deal of fun so far. Though things are looking up. I think he'll love the gags I've got for his big speech tomorrow.

Liz   I look forward to rolling in the aisles. (*To both.*) Now if you'll excuse me.

She makes to leave. **Paul** *stops hers.*

Paul   Wait a minute. Please. (*Turns to* **Simon**.) Simon, would you mind terribly if you used the bathroom for a few minutes?

Simon   Oh, I need a shit again, do I?

Paul   Well . . . yes.

Simon *heads to the bathroom.*

Simon   I have to say, this is not how I envisaged my contribution to the party. (*About to exit, turns.*) I'm doing this for DL and for nobody else. (*Leaves.*)

Paul (*to* **Liz**)   Are you serious? About not publishing?

Liz   Yes.

Paul   You . . . you really ought to publish.

Liz   Oooh-er. Which side are you on?

Paul   I just think you should publish.

Liz   Why's that?

Paul   Look. I was really hoping . . . I really hoped you wouldn't do a deal in there.

Liz   Well, that could mean . . . that could mean the whole house of cards coming down.

Paul   Maybe that wouldn't matter. If it stopped Eddie. He sort of scares me. It's like he doesn't have any limits any more. I think he ought to be stopped.

Liz   And you want me to do the stopping.

Paul   Well, why not?

Liz   Because I've cut my deal. It isn't very attractive. It isn't at all heroic. But I've cut my deal.

Paul   He's a bastard.

Liz   I know. I lived with him.

Paul   No, I mean the Prime Minister. He's a bastard too.

Liz   Yes, I think he probably is.

Paul   So why do the deal?

Liz   Because there's a chance he'll come through. And then I'll have achieved something.

Simon (*off*)   Have I finished yet?

Paul   No! (*To* **Liz**.) The repeal of one bill. Not that big an achievement, is it?

Liz   I've been a campaigning journalist for most of my life, Paul. How much do you think I've achieved.

Paul   Lots, you've achieved lots.

Liz   Wrong. You don't know what it's like. You research and you write and then if you're lucky it gets printed and if you're really lucky it gets printed exactly as you wrote it, and a few liberal friends and colleagues call you up and say 'Great piece, Liz' and if you're really really lucky there's a question in the House and the minister has to obfuscate for a few minutes, and if you're unbelievably supremely lucky the PM sets up a task force on the issue and puts some loser in charge of it and the whole thing goes off the boil and then

. . . well, then it's all over, and you don't really know whether you've achieved anything or not.

Paul   But you have, you know you have.

Liz   No. Eddie's right. The power's always somewhere else. And if you're suddenly in a position to get rid of an Act of Parliament – a particularly nasty Act of Parliament, as it happens – well, then . . . you cut a deal.

Simon (*off*)   I'm coming out, all right?

Paul   No!

Simon (*off*)   Why not?

Paul   We . . . we . . .

Liz   We haven't got our clothes back on yet!

Simon (*off*)   Oh God.

We hear the door being double-locked.

Paul   What makes you think he'll keep his promise?

Liz   If he doesn't, I'll publish.

Paul   It won't be like that. You're locked into old models. Black and white. Good and bad. Right and wrong. That's how he took over the party. DL doesn't keep promises, but he doesn't break them either. He just erodes them. So you'll never be sure when you've been betrayed. Only each day you'll give him the benefit of the doubt, because you need to believe, until one day, there's nothing left. That's how it works.

Liz   Is that what's happened to you?

Paul   I don't know. Yes, probably . . . My daughter . . . she's in hospital in France. After a car accident.

Liz   Oh, I'm sorry. Is it . . . very –?

Paul   No, no, she'll be fine. We've spoken on the phone. And her mother's there. She'll be okay.

Liz   You've not gone out there?

Paul   I'm needed here. The speech . . . and everything.
The thing is, Eddie tried to stop me finding out.

Liz   He didn't want you to know your daughter was
injured?

Paul   That's right.

Liz   God.

Paul   I only found out because George told me.

Liz (*absorbing this*)   Eddie decided the speech came first.

Paul   Yes . . . Well, maybe it does.

Liz   Do you really think that?

Simon (*off*)   Can I come out now?

Liz   I've got to go.

She makes to leave. **Paul** *takes the floppy from* **Eddie**'*s jacket, holds
it out to her. She hesitates.*

Paul   The floppy.

Liz   You could take it, couldn't you? Hand it over to the
press. Couldn't be easier.

Paul   I . . . I can't. I can't do it.

Liz   No, I thought not.

*He keeps holding it up. She stares at it. She finally takes it. Slips it into
her bag. Takes a few steps towards the door.*

Liz (*towards bathroom door*)   We're finished having sex now,
Simon. (*To* **Paul**.) Bye.

Paul   Bye.

Paul *takes himself a coffee, sits down. The doors to the PM's suite
open.* **Eddie** *backs out, a yellow sheet of lined paper in his hand.*

Eddie   I understand your concern, Prime Minister. It'll be your best conference speech ever, and that's a promise. (*Closes doors, and his manner changes dramatically.*) God, that man can be difficult.

Paul (*cheerfully*)   Went well then, did it?

Eddie   Be careful. Be very careful.

Simon *comes out of bathroom.*

Eddie   What are you doing out?

Simon   I'm sorry. I'm tired of being told I need a shit. There are limits, you know.

Eddie   Shut up and get back in there.

Simon   Yes, all right. (*Half-leaves, turns.*) It isn't like this at Chequers, is it?

Eddie (*as if scaring off a pigeon*)   Waaaahhh!

Simon *jumps with fear, disappears back into the bathroom, closes the door.* **Eddie** *throws down yellow lined sheet on table.*

Eddie   DL's very worried about the press reaction to repealing the Asylum Act. He thinks we could lose Murdoch on this one.

Paul (*ironic*)   Oh, we mustn't let that happen, must we?

Eddie   He'll announce the decision to repeal the act, but we've somehow got to word it so that it sounds like a firm measure. (*Refers to sheet.*) Look. Firm but fair. Not a soft touch.

Paul   This is a bit of a challenge, isn't it?

Eddie   We can do it. Let's get going.

Paul   I don't feel like it. Do it yourself.

Eddie   Don't do this, Paul. I don't need this.

Paul   I think it's vile how you treated Liz. I think she ought to publish. And if she doesn't, maybe I'll do something about it. You were right, of course. I do keep a diary.

Eddie   Oh yeah?

Eddie *grabs him, puts one arm up his back.*

Paul   Eddie, what're you doing? Eddie, you're hurting my arm!

Eddie   Oh, am I? I'm so sorry. I just wanted to explain something to you, you see, I know all about your little friend Steve. Pretty little Steve.

Paul   So what. Not illegal, is it?

Eddie   Well, no, it isn't illegal, though it's not my idea of fun. (*Viciously slams* **Paul** *forward across the table.*) But how you first met? That wasn't so sweet, was it? Both arrested for gross indecency. Cottaging. What a romantic start to a relationship. What did you do, fuck him in the holding cells?

Simon *emerges from bathroom.*

Simon   Excuse me – (*Takes in the scene, with* **Eddie** *pressed over* **Paul**'s *back.*)

Eddie   Or do you prefer taking it?

Simon   Oh my God!

Simon *quickly goes back into bathroom, slams door.*

Eddie   How's your daughter going to feel if she finds the story all over the newspapers next week? I can't imagine it'll improve your chances of seeing her more often. Can you?

Paul   You're breaking my fucking arm!

Eddie *lets go.*

Paul   Maybe . . . maybe she won't be bothered by any of that. Maybe she'll be more bothered that I worked with bastards like you, helped keep this fucking government in power.

Eddie   She'll be making this insightful choice aged eight, will she? Is that how old she is, eight?

Paul   Seven.

Eddie   Seven. And in the playground do you think they'll be making jokes about the government, or jokes about her dad? Think about it, Paul. And keep your mouth shut. Now write the speech. And make it good. Oh, and you'll hand over those diaries soon as we get back to London.

Asha *enters from the corridor, carrying a man's dark blue suit on a hanger with a dry-cleaner's transparent cover. She also has a selection of five or six ties on a little rack. She hangs up suit and ties somewhere on the set (over back of a chair?).*

Asha   It's a bit of a shambles down there. Some protestors got inside the hotel.

Eddie (*to* **Asha**)   In the hotel! How's that possible?

Asha   I don't know, Eddie. I'm not in charge of security. But the Home Secretary wasn't impressed. Got knocked over by two Group Four men chasing a woman down a corridor.

Eddie   That shouldn't happen!

Asha   Well, that's a useful insight, isn't it? I think we all know it shouldn't happen. (*She selects ties, considering them.*) Oh, tiny problem with tomorrow's ordinary people, Eddie. The granny who's beaten loneliness fell down and broke her hip. Three days ago.

Eddie   Shit.

Asha   I sort of assumed you must know about it.

Eddie   It's not a problem. Paul, we need an upbeat granny by tomorrow lunchtime.

Paul   Oh, great.

Asha   Apparently she was left for ages on a trolley before she got seen.

Eddie   Make sure that doesn't come out, okay?

Asha   It's out. Tomorrow's *Mail*. 'My 50 hours of NHS hell, by Conference granny'.

Eddie   Fuck.

Asha   Oh, and the self-made millionaire has just filed for bankruptcy.

Eddie   Aw, Christ! Who's that leave? Let me see . . .

Eddie *finds the gum on his chair, peels it off, throws it away in a fury. Phone rings.* **Paul** *answers it upstage.*

Asha   The nurse, the junior doctor, the head teacher, the graphic designer and the bloke in the wheelchair. That'll be fine.

Eddie   No, it won't be fine! It needs the granny and it needs the millionaire! It's a very delicate balance. We can find a millionaire. Paul, get the list of invitees to last night's fund-raising dinner. And this town is brimming over with grannies. There must be one of them has beaten loneliness.

Paul *(phone in hand, with a sense of Schadenfreude)*   Eddie. It's the *Sun*. They want to know if you'll comment on the cleaner who got fired.

Eddie   Who is it? Is it Trevor?

Paul   Yes.

Eddie   Tell him she was pilfering. They were going to bring the police in, but I overruled. I felt sorry for her. I'm hurt she's not more grateful.

Paul   You tell him.

Eddie   Christ. How can we make anything work if you keep . . . defying me?!

Paul   Maybe I don't want to make anything work.

Eddie   Oh, fucking grow up!

Asha   Men don't do that, do they?

Off: whooping sound of an alarm in the hotel.

Paul   Fire alarm?

Asha   No, security alert.

Paul   Bit late, isn't it?

Simon *comes out of the bathroom.*

Simon   Do we have to evacuate?

Eddie   No! But you do! Get back in there!

Simon   Yes. Okay. Sorry.

He goes back in, closes the door.
The bathroom door opens again, **Simon** *comes out.*

Simon   Sorry. No. There are limits. I'm not prepared to die in a fire just for the sake of the party.

Asha   It's not a fire!

Simon   I think it's time I was treated with a bit of respect round here. I've been invited to Chequers, you know.

The whooping of the alarm stops.

Asha   Oh good. The fire is over.

Paul   Hello, Trevor. Eddie says he couldn't give a fuck.

Eddie (*to* **Paul**)   Give me that phone!

Paul   No.

Eddie (*grabbing it*)   Give it here!

Paul   No!

They fight over possession of the phone.

Asha   What's the matter with you two?

Simon (*to* **Asha**)   Lovers' quarrel.

Asha   Uh?

Eddie (*into phone, while pushing* **Paul** *away*)   Trevor, it's Eddie. She was pilfering.

Paul *grabs it back.*

Paul (*into phone*)   No she wasn't!

Eddie *grabs it back.*

Eddie   Sorry about that, Trevor.

The door bursts opens and **George** *crashes in, his hair, face and shirt covered in brown and cream gunk.*

George   There are lesbians in the dining room! I was . . . I was just having a word with the maître d' when two ghastly women in pullovers came running past and pushed profiteroles in my face. (*Wipes gunk from his face.*) I'm sorry, what kind of society do we live in? And more to the point, what the fuck do the police think they're doing?! (*Moves awkwardly across to the balcony windows, peers out cautiously.*) Look at that. Why don't they use water cannons on the bastards?

Asha   Are you injured?

George   No.

Asha   You're limping.

George   Well, if you really want to know, they also pushed profiteroles down my trousers.

George *crosses to the recliner.*

Eddie   Don't sit there! Trevor, Listen . . .

George   This isn't the right to protest, is it? This is anarchy.

George *sits down heavily on the recliner, his hands smearing cream and chocolate over it. From his trousers he excavates more profiteroles, dumps them on the recliner.* **Asha**'s *and* **Eddie**'s *bleepers go. They both look at them.*

Asha   It's DL. He needs me.

Eddie   And me. (*Into phone.*) I'll get back to you, Trevor
. . . uh? No . . . (*Sees* **Asha** *heading towards PM's door.*) . . .
Look, drop the fired cleaner story and I'll tell you where one
of DL's kids is clubbing tomorrow night . . . Okay? Right,
it's Chill City . . . Brixton . . . Yeah. Very sleazy, very
druggy. (*Puts phone down, heads off in same direction as* **Asha**.)

George *stands up, stares outside. The noises of rioting grow louder.*

George   It's horribly rough out there.

Eddie (*stares at the recliner. To* **George**)   You've . . . covered
. . . my recliner with . . . profiteroles. You fuckwit! (*Realises
floppy isn't in jacket.*) Where's the floppy? Where's the floppy
that Liz brought?

Paul   She took it away again.

Eddie   She's not planning to renege on the deal, is she?

Paul   Yes. I think probably she is.

Eddie   Is she still in the hotel?

Paul   No idea.

Eddie   I need to find her!

*There is a loud crash of breaking glass as an object flies through the
balcony doors and lands about centre stage, not far from George. All
freeze for a moment. The object makes a hissing noise. They all stare at
it.* **George** *approaches it.*

George   What the hell's this? It's . . . it's not tear gas, is it?
(*Picks it up.*) Do you know, I think it might be tear gas.

George *panics, and throws it into the centre of the room. All stare at
it for a moment.*

Simon   It's . . . it's enough to make you weep . . . Haaa!
(*Pause.*) Sorry.

*The tear-gas canister explodes. The suite fills with smoke. The smoke
alarms go off. There is confusion as everybody, coughing and choking,
makes for the exit.*

Triumphal orchestral music surges forth.

Blackout.

Scene Three

The triumphal music continues as the previous set is transformed into a conference stage: basically a lectern plus autocue screens and a giant screen or set of monitors for projecting video pictures of the person at the lectern.

The smoke of the tear gas becomes the dry ice of a showbizzy political presentation. Lights shine out through the smoke into the auditorium as the music grows in volume.

On a big screen, a video runs, showing **DL** *'backstage' at Conference, as he prepares to make his big entrance. He is accompanied by* **Eddie**, **Asha** *and security men.*

Massive applause as **DL** *makes his entrance.*

Lights up on **DL** *at the lectern. The audience in the theatre now becomes his Conference audience.*

DL   Thank you . . . Thank you . . . (*He 'modestly' gestures for the applause to stop. Pauses.*) A couple of hours ago, I had a big speech ready for this moment. And then, because of the extraordinary and shocking events of the last twenty-four hours, I decided to tear it up. To throw away the fine phrases that other people were urging me to use. And to talk to you directly, simply, spontaneously, from the heart. (*Pauses, looks around his audience.*) You know, it's weird. Sometimes it feels like being Prime Minister is a job that's different from any other job. And in a way it is. Well, for a start, there aren't many other jobs where every week you get to meet three or four presidents, a couple of kings and queens and a few hundred MPs. Except maybe if you're Charlotte Church. (*Laughter.*) But you know, it is different from any other job. Because it carries more responsibility than any other job. And sometimes it can be tough.

Sometimes it means you don't have as much family time as you'd like, and you worry about the kids, and you worry about the future. You sometimes even worry about the Deputy Prime Minister! Well, would *you* want to be on the same train as him?!

Laughter, then applause.

But seriously, let's look at the big picture for a moment. Let me tell you something. There are now six billion human beings on the planet. Today 230,000 people will be born. Every day, the human race growing by the equivalent of the city of Sunderland. Every month a London. Every year another Germany. Just think: 230,000 children born today. And shall I tell you how many of those children will grow up in the developing world, where millions go hungry? (*Long pause.*) Ninety-seven per cent. And we can't avoid the question: how are they to be fed? Yes, we can talk about reforming the world bank. Yes, we can talk about modernising the IMF. Yes, we can talk about debt relief. Yes, we can talk about changes to the World Trade Organisation. But what's going to feed the hungry is not talk, not meetings, not fine words from the world's politicians. (*Forcefully.*) And certainly not anarchy and rioting in our streets.

Applause.

No, what's going to feed the hungry is, quite literally, food. (*Between thumb and forefinger he holds up a grain of rice.*) I want you to look at this. If you can see it. (*Smiles.*) It's a grain of rice. Rice. The staple food of half the world's population. What could be more ordinary? But this grain of rice has been genetically modifed to grow at five times the speed of normal rice. So it could transform the lives and prospects of the world's poor. A modern miracle. The feeding of the five thousand. No loaves. No fishes. Just this grain of rice. That's the reality of GM foods. That's the promise of GM crops. Just imagine: a new age of plenty for all humanity. Of course, there will be opposition. People who say no to the

future. People who say to hell with the new advances in
genetic engineering. To hell with the needs of the Third
World. To hell with the hungry. These are the forces of the
past. And shall I tell you something? (*Pauses, then his tone goes
strident.*) The forces of the past were out on the streets of this
town last night, looting and burning and destroying!

Loud applause.

And they think there isn't a price to pay in human life. But
of course, there always is. And there was. An innocent life.
When a wing of this town's most historic hotel was torched
in the early hours of this morning, it wasn't a member of the
government who died. It was an innocent journalist.
Someone quietly going about her job of providing us with
the information, the opinions, the insights, which are the
very oxygen of democracy. I may not have agreed with
every word she wrote, but I can never forgive those who
have silenced her voice for ever. When the perpetrators of
this evil deed are arrested – as they surely will be – and
when we introduce new measures to make sure they go to
prison and stay in prison – as we surely shall – and when we
take steps to outlaw this kind of anarchy on our streets – as
we firmly intend to do – then there will be voices of
complaint. Voices talking about freedom and liberty and the
right to demonstrate. And do you know what I say to them?
I say: what about the freedom of ordinary decent people to
walk down the street without being terrorised by looters,
thugs and anarchists?!

Thunderous applause.

What about the ordinary decent people who want to do an
honest day's work for an honest day's pay? The people who
wonder – quite rightly – why young people who refuse to
work should be pampered and cosseted and allowed to run
wild on our streets? Those are the people I care about. The
people who say to me, what we want is a job culture, not a
yob culture.

You know, we have a great tradition of tolerence in this country. It's a decent country. A humane country. A country that's always given a welcome to those fleeing genuine persecution in other parts of the globe. Genuine persecution. To the bogus, the cheats, the economic migrants, the traders in human misery, I say, you will not find this country a soft touch!

Applause.

Which is why, in the next session of Parliament, we will bring in new measures to tighten up on bogus asylum seekers!

Loud applause.

That's part of our global responsibility too. This government has never shrunk from its global responsibilities. And it won't shrink from them now, even if it means short-term unpopularity.

There's so much more I'd wanted to say. But sometimes, you know, even as Prime Minister, you can't do exactly as you want. There are injured people to visit in hospital. There are members of our brave emergency services to be thanked. There's a meeting with the Home Secretary to draw up details of our new security measures. But we do these things in a spirit of hope. With our eyes on tomorrow, not yesterday. Because this is the party of hope. This is the party of change. This is the party of the future.

Prolonged, stormy applause. **DL** *acknowledges the applause. Waves. Takes in the house. There is a blitz of flashlights. Suddenly the sound snaps off, leaving only a moment of echo.* **DL** *stands alone, frozen in a spotlight as the light slowly fades to black.*

Curtain.

As the company take their curtain calls, we again hear the song 'Feelgood'.